R.

That's Amore!

*Love, lasagne and language trouble
in a 1970s Italian village*

That's Amore!

Love, lasagne and language trouble
in a 1970s Italian village

Matador
9 Priory Business Park,
Wistow Road, Kibworth Beauchamp,
Leicestershire. LE8 0RX
Tel: (+44) 116 279 2299
Fax: (+44) 116 279 2277
Email: books@troubador.co.uk
Web: www.troubador.co.uk/matador

ISBN 978 1783060 634

British Library Cataloguing in Publication Data.
A catalogue record for this book is available from the British Library.

Typeset in 12pt Bembo by Troubador Publishing Ltd, Leicester, UK

Matador is an imprint of Troubador Publishing Ltd

For Mum

Acknowledgments

I'd like to thank my family for their support while I was writing this book. In particular, I'd like to give a special mention to my Mum who was my Number One critic and had the job of reading and re-reading, giving heartfelt comments at the end but who didn't get to see it in print.

Thanks to Gordon Kerr, who gave me invaluable advice and edited the book, calmly talking me through the simplest of problems.

Thanks to my sister-in-law, Debbie Baker who read every chapter I emailed giving me constructive feedback.

Special thanks to Ivan Guglielmana, not only a talented musician but also a computer wizard – and my saviour – who answered every S.O.S. each time I managed to erase an entire file or needed help with some technical problem on the pc while writing.

Thanks to Marco Barbieri for his help in correcting my Italian dialogue and to Katia and Michele Rapella who gave helpful comments regarding various aspects of the book.

A big thank you to Ilaria Martinalli and Francesco Pezzini for finding the right photo for the book cover.

Also thanks to Cristian Colturri, Angela Rossini and Dino Pensa who helped me out with dialect and terminology alien to a foreigner.

Thanks to Julie Schindler who gave me moral support when I needed it over litres of coffee in our favourite Bar in Morbegno.

Lastly, I must thank my husband, Michele for his patience in having to wait for his meals when I'd done something wrong for the umpteenth time and was going ballistic in the study instead of preparing his food in the kitchen. To one and all, I say "Thank You."

Prologue

Intent on polishing the table, I didn't hear the door of the disco open, but the sharp clip of footsteps on the newly laid tiles made me look up. Two tall men wearing expensive dark suits and sunglasses strode purposefully into my vision.

'This is like a scene from *The Godfather*,' I thought as laughter bubbled up in my throat. 'Where's the violin case with a rifle?' Then I noticed that one of them carried a briefcase and suddenly it didn't seem so funny.

I tried to attract Michele's attention but he'd already seen them. Carefully replacing the records he'd been sorting through in the DJ's corner, he made his way towards them, gesturing to them to take a seat around one of the modern blue tables. Exchanging looks, they refused. Then the one carrying the briefcase laid it ceremoniously on the counter of the bar.

'I wish Pietro was here,' I thought. 'Why on earth did he have to go to Morbegno this afternoon?'

Worried about Michele and too far away to see or hear anything clearly, I inched forward in the shadows until I almost tripped over a table. With adrenaline pumping through my body and my heart thumping loudly, I sat down where I was, deciding that maybe I shouldn't interfere after all.

Peering round a chair, I saw Michele offering the Men-in-Black a drink. Fortunately, just at that moment, as they put down their glasses, Pietro arrived. The conversation became quite animated as clipped voices grew in volume and I caught glimpses of gold cufflinks and gold watches when they gestured towards the interior of the Rendez Vous discotheque. These strangers exuded wealth but their body language emanated an element of danger. Both Michele and Pietro shook their heads repeatedly and I almost jumped out of my skin when one of the men slammed his hand down on the counter, the noise echoing around the walls like a warning. I shivered.

They left as quickly as they'd arrived and following them quietly, I just had time to see a sleek, black Mercedes purr down to the bottom of the road. Who were they and what did they want? Deep down, though, I knew the answer.

Michele and Pietro still had their heads together, talking in dialect and didn't hear me when I walked up behind them.

"Have we just had a visit from the local mafia?"

"They're from somewhere near Lake Como and they came specifically to ask if we wanted to pay them *protection money*," Michele explained, as beads of perspiration appeared on his forehead.

"And...?" I had never seen him so apprehensive before.

"And we refused their *kind offer* but now we 'ave to be careful nothing *'appens* to our disco… or us."

"Oh." As the significance of what Michele was saying sank in, I realised that this was for real. My days of boredom in a sleepy mountain village in northern Italy had ended but what would happen now…?

1

1977 – Goodbye England, Hello Italy

'This is it,' I thought to myself as I settled back in my seat next to Michele and fastened my seatbelt. After a delay of two and a half hours spent wandering idly around the shops at Gatwick Airport, we were more than ready to say goodbye to England. As the engines roared in our ears, the plane lurched forward and before we knew it we were above the Sussex coastline.

Michele took out his *Gazzetta dello Sport* and scanned the pages for news of his beloved Fiorentina. Meanwhile, I looked out of the tiny window and had a last view of the English Channel before flying into the clouds. I closed my eyes and daydreamed about snow-capped mountains, spectacular lakes, chalets with verandas furnished with patio chairs and tables laden with cool drinks and snacks.

A heartfelt round of applause from the Italian passengers as we landed woke me from my reverie and brought me back to the present.

"Why did everyone clap?" I asked as we jostled our way off the plane.

"It's just an Italian custom to show we are 'appy for arriving safe and sound," Michele explained with a smile.

Walking across the tarmac to the bus waiting to take us to the terminal, I found myself gasping for breath as the heat roared through the darkness.

"What's the temperature here?"

"Oh, I think the pilot said it's 35°," Michele replied, glad to have left behind the cold English climate he was forever complaining about.

Feeling as though I'd just walked out of a sauna, with my hair and clothes sticking to my body, I now understood why the majority of female passengers had skimpy tops under T-shirts and were busy stripping off. Dressed for a typical British summer in jeans and a thick, long-sleeved T-shirt, I had little option but to suffer in silence.

As we made our way to passport control, I realised not for the last time that queuing and waiting your turn didn't apply to Italians. Bodies pushed and shoved in front of us, attempting to be first in line and elbows proved to be an effective means of eliminating any obstacles, as I painfully found out. Rubbing my ribs where an immaculately dressed woman had found her target, I tried without much success to stand up to the surging mass behind me. Conversation grew louder and more animated.

"Why do Italians seem to shout when they open their mouths?" I whispered to Michele.

"We don't shout. It's you English that speak quietly."

'Oh,' I thought to myself and just as I was going to say something else, a middle-aged couple trying to reach friends at the head of the queue literally propelled us out of the way.

"*Scusate, ci fate passare?*"

"*Prego*," Michele replied, stepping aside.

"What did they say?"

"They asked if we could let them pass and I said 'please'. That's what we say instead of 'certainly'."

"Aha." I stored '*prego*' for future reference.

The fact that I could understand no Italian whatsoever apart from the standard: *sì, no* and *grazie*, did not deter me. With Michele beside me, I felt confident enough to believe that I would learn the language easily and quickly.

"I need a coffee, an Italian one," Michele said with feeling while waiting for our cases. We headed for the nearest bar.

The strong and bitter *espresso* almost scalded my tonsils as I swallowed the contents in two gulps. Twenty minutes later, as we took our seats on the coach to take us to the station, Michele looked worriedly at his watch.

"I 'ope we don't miss the last train from Milan to Morbegno."

We did, but whereas Michele couldn't wait to get home, it meant I had a few more hours to prepare myself. I felt excited but also scared. After a cappuccino and a *brioche* from the only kiosk open at that late hour at Milan's Central Station, we had no alternative but to wait for the first early morning train. In those days, wasting money on a hotel room was not an option. Although I hadn't expected to spend my first night on Italian soil lying on top of our cases on a noisy platform in the company of bored cleaners, passengers waiting impatiently for their trains and hungry pigeons, with Michele's arms protectively around me and his promise of a new life together in my ears, I still felt happy and excited.

*

The train to Morbegno left at five in the morning and I couldn't wait to get some proper sleep. Imagine my disappointment, therefore, when I discovered, instead of the cushioned seats used by British Rail, nothing but hard wooden benches. Unable to talk above the noise of the locomotive, I looked at Michele sleeping peacefully beside me, his head rocking gently against the window.

I confess I had a moment of weakness, wondering whether Italy was as wonderful as Michele had made out, as a wave of tiredness enveloped me and a numbness in my *derrière* made it increasingly difficult for me to find a comfy position. Finding it impossible to doze, I let my mind wander back over the last eighteen months – eighteen months that had completely changed my life.

*

I met Michele during my second year at the East Sussex College of Education in Eastbourne. My student friends and I worked as waitresses in the Lounge at the Grand Hotel at weekends serving afternoon teas, and Michele was in charge. His black wavy hair and olive skin emphasised his Mediterranean looks. Watching him in his immaculate uniform, head held high, giving short, clipped orders one moment in his alluring and inimitable English, then leaning down to share a few words with elderly guests sipping their tea, stirred something in the recesses of my heart. That primal emotion grew stronger every time he caught me looking at him and smiled into my eyes. Until then, I'd always preferred dating English men because I had no intention of leaving my family or home or giving up my dreams of becoming a teacher, but with Michele I suffered an acute form of amnesia. From our first *cappuccino* together in a local café after work, I fell helplessly and uncontrollably in love with him, selfishly enjoying this new intimacy. Day after day, I attended lectures and prepared lessons for teaching practice, while Michele served morning coffee and afternoon tea at the hotel. He came to fetch me at my student digs at the same time every evening and my heart always skipped a beat when I heard the familiar voice ask one of my friends: "Is Val ready?"

We spent our evenings in the disco where he helped to collect glasses, secretly noting everything that made a disco unique: the lighting, the dance floor, the music. If he closed his eyes, he could visualise his very own dream disco and he never tired of describing it to me.

When I introduced him to my family and friends, they realised from our continual eye contact and intimate smiles that ours was a special relationship and no one was surprised when, a year later, we decided to move into a flat together. During our frequent weekends in Poole, they listened with genuine interest as Michele talked about the village where his family lived in the house his father had built in the late 1950s, and the dream he shared with Pietro, his brother, to build a disco. For once, I didn't bore everyone with the latest pedagogical theories I'd studied. In fact, I didn't mention anything concerning teaching. No one actually voiced the inevitable question: what's going to happen next? But everyone sensed that change was in the air.

The phone call came while I was studying furiously for my finals in May. Practically falling through the door, Michele could hardly get the words out quickly enough.

"Pietro rang the hotel. I 'ave to go to Italy for a week to decide on the design of the disco. *Sì,* they passed the plans. *E' incredibile!*" I'd never seen him so excited.

Their friend, Adriano had just graduated in construction engineering and so his very first job was to build a discotheque. While Adriano pored over plans in Italy, back in Eastbourne, we spent our evenings discussing our future which now took a different turn. Up to then, we'd talked about our dreams, both egotistically believing they'd come true without either of us having to make any sacrifices but with the disco becoming a reality, I had to decide there and then whether I wanted to make Italy my home. Michele had promised Pietro that he would go back in July. I would have finished my exams, but if I followed him, I would have to forget about staying on for another year to get my Bachelor of Education degree and a career in a classroom. Did I love him enough to give up my dream of teaching and maybe, like my father, become a head teacher? I loved teaching young children more than anything else, seeing their expressions of sheer delight when they learned and understood something new or helping them overcome difficulties with reading and writing. I enjoyed the challenges within the classroom during our months of teaching practice and up to then nothing could crush my aspiration of joining the ranks of dedicated teachers – until Michele walked into my life.

"It's possible you teach in Italy," Michele suggested, as we walked slowly back to our flat one evening. I'd gone to meet him after spending a pensive hour on the beach watching the waves roll lazily over the pebbles, trying to imagine life away from my family and the sea but at the same time, as the gentle lapping echoed in my ears, I couldn't envisage life without Michele.

"We're near Lake Como, you know," he added, pulling me to him and kissing me softly.

"Certainly, it's not the sea but it's still water." I had to laugh. To him, every problem had a solution and there was nothing to worry about: we loved each other and wanted to be together. The fact that his dream disco evolving in Italy meant I had to rethink my dream of teaching in the U.K. just wasn't an issue. He was usually quite a sensitive person, but this time I saw a determination in him that wouldn't be easily swayed. If I decided to spend the rest of my life with him, then I'd have to follow him to Italy.

Sleepless nights didn't solve my dilemma and Michele fussed over my tired face and aching head. Always indecisive at the best of times, I felt the twang of heartstrings being pulled to the limit: I wanted to be with Michele but I also wanted to be with my family and to teach. I don't know how long this yo-yo situation would have continued if it hadn't been for a conversation I had with Michele's friend from Sondrio who also worked at the Grand Hotel.

"If you love Michele," Ivan said in his appealing Italian accent, "then go wiv 'im. Otherwise, stay 'ere wiv me," he added with a wink.

Sound advice. I decided to follow my heart. The next weekend, Michele and I went to Poole to tell the family.

For the past nine years, since the premature death of our father at the age of 43, we'd become a close-knit clan with an unspoken code of sibling unity. How would they react to my news? I needn't have worried. My Mum's response was: "If you've made up your mind, then I'm not going to make you change it. I just want you to be happy." My sister relished the prospect of holidays in Italy and my grandparents and aunt, although surprised, knew I'd never do anything without careful thought. I secretly needed my brother's approval. He'd become the man of the house and although I hadn't always appreciated his protectiveness in the past, especially when he wanted to know where I was going on a

Saturday night or who I was seeing, I now realised that he'd acted on impulse, feeling genuinely responsible for all of us. His fiancée understood my predicament and in her quiet manner, pointed out that Italy wasn't as far away as America or Australia. I had a mixture of reactions from friends who after the initial shock, like my sister, said they'd come to visit.

Michele had never actually proposed in the traditional way but it was a foregone conclusion that we would marry.

"We'll have to get engaged and you have to buy me an engagement ring."

"What?" Michele spluttered. "Why do you need a ring before we marry? We 'ave to save all our money for the disco."

"No ring, no wedding, no Italy!" My tone left no doubts that I meant it.

"Okay. And I suppose you already chose the ring?"

The following afternoon, ignoring the lack of dialogue on his part, I marched him into the jewellers and pointed to the designated love token. Blinking at the simple diamond set in a thin gold band, glittering in the artificial lighting, and noting the price, his face broke into a smile. I declined the assistant's offer of placing my engagement ring in a showy box and, deftly slipping the small solitaire on my third finger, I practically floated out of the shop.

"Now you're my fiancé!" I gave him a quick kiss.

He gave me a quizzical look before guiding me to our local café to celebrate over a *cappuccino*.

As in most classic romantic films and novels, love defeats all obstacles, and so it did in my case. Hoping that I wouldn't regret my decision, and despite my tutor's advice to stay on for the fourth year and taking the degree for my own satisfaction and self-esteem, I thanked him, said goodbye to my family and friends, packed my essential belongings in a brand new case, and on 3rd July, 1977, I left England with Michele.

And now, twenty-four hours later, here I was on an old, decidedly uncomfortable train, rattling noisily to Morbegno, desperately pushing all negative thoughts to the back of my mind. Stealing another look at him, a wave of unconditional love welled up inside me and as I lay my head on his shoulder, I remembered one of our afternoons sitting on the hot pebbles on the beach at Eastbourne.

"Tell me about the Valtellina," I'd said.

"Well, it's a valley in the mountains where we grow corn and fruit, and grapes for our famous wines. You see the vineyards from the main road to Sondrio – that's the county town – rows and rows of them, with their names on large signs. *E' spettacolare.*" His eyes had a faraway look and he was already back in his hometown, speaking Italian.

"There are a few ski resorts near us for people who want to 'ave a 'oliday during the winter, we call those 'olidays *la Settimana Bianca* or White Week. We go there one day, maybe." His voice trailed off as he took his time lighting a cigarette. "And there are lots of walks in the mountains with shelters to spend the night. Certainly, it's a rural place, it's quiet, not noisy like Milan. And not like Poole, it's much quieter. The people are different, too. They are simple people, farming people." He added as an afterthought.

And I am about to meet them. I gulped. Reality loomed like a dark cloud of bleak uncertainty. What would they think of me? Or more to the point, what would I think of them?

Just as my stomach started to feel as if I'd swallowed a blender, a kind of idyllic picture postcard scene unfolded before my eyes. I prodded Michele, who waking with a jolt, realised where we were and proudly introduced me to Lake Como with the mountains, *his* green mountains, surrounding it. Villages materialised around the lakeside and some appeared to go further up the Alps. Sunlight glinted on cars weaving along the roads, occasionally disappearing from view as they headed higher and higher through the aging pines. Each village, with houses of different shapes and sizes, built on any available land, had its own church which occupied a strategic position. The numbness and stiffness in my body disappeared.

"Why are there so many villages high up the mountains? They seem totally inaccessible and in this day and age, who would choose to live up a mountain anyway?"

"The *Valtellinesi*," replied my fiancé, as if it were obvious. "In the past, people lived at the top of the mountains. 'Ave a look, they form a circle. You see? During the summer months, they took their animals to the summit so they could get the best milk. That meant the families 'ad the tastiest fresh milk, cream, butter and cheese."

Now in his element, Michele went on to explain that these farming folk lived in ramshackle huts, making do with the bare necessities.

"What, no running water? No bathroom? No shower? What did they do when they needed to wash or go to the loo?" I cringed.

"They used the nearest stream or water in a bucket brought up from the stream to wash and they each 'ad their own spot for relieving themselves."

"Actually," he added "Some people, who take their cows as 'igh as possible, still live in such places in July and August."

I decided there'd be no question of me going up a mountain for a weekend.

Leaving the lake behind us, we followed more small villages and towns sprawling unevenly at the foot of the mountains and fields burnt by the hot relentless summer sun.

"Why aren't there any animals in the fields?" I asked after a while.

"Because they're up the mountains, I just told you," Michele laughed. "The animals won't come down until the middle of October."

It seemed strange to me to see great expanses of empty grassland. I nearly shouted out in delight when I spotted several horses grazing in a field.

"You can see the river Adda from my parents' 'ouse.

If you look carefully, you should see their 'ouse in a minute. It's a grey stone one with a red roof."

With our noses pressed to the window-pane, we strained to get a glimpse of the place where Michele had spent his first sixteen years.

"There it is!"

The house appeared to be built on its own with woodland behind it. A few houses stood a short distance away to the left and a three-storey house loomed below it. The latter belonged to Michele's aunt and uncle.

Almost at the same moment a strong, sweet smell of biscuits filled our nostrils.

"Look on your right, that's the famous *Galbusera* factory that makes the best biscuits around. Their products are sent all over Italy and abroad as well."

Three minutes later we rumbled slowly into Morbegno station.

"We need a cool drink before taking a taxi to Piussogno," Michele said, leading the way to a group of tables outside a bar opposite the station. When I raised my eyebrows at the mention of a taxi, wondering how much it would cost, Michele explained: "There are only two buses a day: one in the morning and one in the afternoon."

"Ah," I preferred not to dwell on that latest piece of information. I knew Piussogno couldn't be referred to as a metropolis but I didn't think it was that isolated.

Michele ordered two fruit juices and two *brioche*s and while sipping my peach juice, I glimpsed a little part of Italian life in the square. Chubby middle-aged women carrying heavy shopping bags trudged past to catch a bus; stylish younger women tottering on open-toed stilettos and chatting animatedly to each other made their way to the car park. Harassed mothers with buggies pushed by with purpose, ignoring the cries of their offspring. Then I saw an elderly woman who appeared to be in fancy dress.

"She's wearing the traditional costume of Mello, a mountain village not far from Piussogno and certainly, it's not a common sight," Michele informed me.

She wore a long, black dress with what seemed to be a coloured scarf over her shoulders with the ends tucked into a decorative apron tied around her ample waist. A headscarf knotted at the back of her neck covered her head and her feet, encased in a pair of clogs, clattered along the uneven cobbles. Just as the woman walked slowly out of sight, a car rounded the corner.

"Look at that. It's just like a bubble car - but it's so small."

"It's a Fiat *cinquecento*," Michele enlightened me. "Fiat 500s are very popular."

With that, another two went by, so they had to have something going for them. One actually had a convertible roof and the driver had one hand on the steering wheel and the other was beating time in the air to the familiar strains of a Beatles' song blaring out from the car radio. This particular Fiat 500 appeared to whiz along, whereas the other, driven by an older person, coughed and spluttered on aching axles.

Mopeds seemed popular, too. People zipped along on

them – and, I noticed, with no crash helmets. At that moment, several cars passed slowly in quick succession and I could see quite clearly that none of the drivers had fastened their seatbelts.

"Hey, how come those drivers aren't wearing seatbelts? Isn't it against the law to drive without?"

Michele took a bite of his *brioche* before answering.

"This is Italy. There's no law saying you 'ave to wear seatbelts. Cars don't even 'ave them."

While Michele paid the bill, I asked to use the bathroom and had another shock. Firstly, there was no distinction between Men and Women and secondly: where was the toilet? All I found was a ceramic slab with a place for your feet and a hole. I only hoped this was a one off.

"You might have warned me," I hissed as Michele guided me out onto the pavement.

"What are you talking about?"

"The toilet!"

"Oh, was it a 'ole?"

"Yes, it was."

End of conversation.

A lone taxi waited patiently for a customer and when its owner saw us marching purposefully towards him, he stubbed out his cigarette and greeted us with a hearty: "*Salve.*" He threw our cases unceremoniously into the boot and we settled into the back of the car. Michele gave him our destination and off we went. Having almost knocked down a couple of pedestrians on the zebra crossing, we ignored the red traffic light and drove straight on, narrowly missing a car which, in fact, had right of way. A screeching of brakes heralded another near miss, this time with an old man on a bike wobbling dangerously with two bulging plastic bags on his handlebars. Our driver kept up a constant flow of conversation, completely oblivious to the fact that we weren't too impressed with his ability to drive and Michele's hand on mine was not a sign of affection but an effort to reassure me that we would live to see another day.

As we left the town behind us, Michele pointed out an ancient bridge over the river Adda. Fields of varying shades spread in front of us before a sign announced La Valletta, a locality in a village called Traona. Houses with red and grey roofs sat haphazardly between fenced off pieces of land, barns and stables. We passed a school, some shops, and a cemetery.

"'Ere we are," Michele announced, "Piussogno."

A few houses lined each side of the road and I could just make out the church to the right. Suddenly we turned off the main road and followed a narrow road towards a fountain. Another right turn and we ran out of tarmac. 'Help!' I thought, 'where are we going?' A sudden knot in my stomach replaced my initial excitement.

The taxi literally bounced over a beaten track with a couple of old, grey stone houses on the left and fields on the right.

"Look, that's my dad's vineyard," Michele pointed out. "And that one belongs to my uncle. Oh, there's my aunt. *Ciao, zia!*"

A robust woman wearing a headscarf, bent double working on the vines, straightened up and shaded her eyes to focus on the person calling to her. On identifying him, she waved her arms about, shouting something completely unintelligible to me.

Within moments, people appeared from nowhere to follow our slow progress over the rough ground. I didn't really take much notice of them. I was too busy trying to work out what my future home was going to look like. Michele waved and shouted to each in turn, occasionally naming them for me. One last tight corner, which took quite a lot of manoeuvring and the taxi shuddered to a halt. The front door of the house in front of us opened and a short, rotund woman wearing a headscarf and a sleeveless overall ran towards Michele and hugged him before standing back and taking a long, hard look at me. Not quite knowing how to react to her intense stare, I smiled back limply. A man I recognised from the photographs Michele had shown me as his father, followed her, puffing away on a cigarette. A young, female version of Michele came running down some steps to the side of the house. Without further ado, I had my first initiation of a true Italian welcome as his parents, Carla and Alberto and youngest sister, Mara hugged and kissed me.

"Ah, *Valeria, Valeria,*" repeated his mother.

"Why is she calling me *Valeria*? My name's Valerie," I whispered to Michele.

"She likes the name '*Valeria*'," said Michele. "Anyway, that's what it is in Italian."

To me, it sounded too much like malaria but I decided it would probably be best not to antagonise my future mother-in-law five minutes after arriving. I vowed to put the record straight in time.

By now, the group had joined us.

"Why is everyone looking at my stomach?" I hadn't eaten much for the past twenty-four hours, so it was more than flat.

"I'll tell you later." Michele knew that bringing a foreigner home could only mean one thing to the villagers – I was in the family way. Totally oblivious to this notion, I rewarded everyone with the warmest of smiles, even allowing them to kiss me on both cheeks as friends and relatives who just happened to be in the vicinity introduced themselves. Then, one by one they drifted off to their respective jobs and Michele, lifting both our cases, invited me to follow him into the house. Taking a deep breath, and returning his smile, I walked into my new life at 18, Via Fiesso.

2

Weak Tea and Red Wine

The next few days passed in a blur of mixed emotions as I came to terms with life in a mountain village. I found the tranquility of the place a welcome change to the frenetic pace of a busy urban town in England but the intense heat and huge black flies with their incessant buzzing, not to mention the mosquitoes, I could do without.

When I walked into the house for the first time, it took a while for my eyes to adapt to the dimly lit interior. The closed shutters kept the rooms cool but also dark. As soon as Mara pulled up the shutters by a cord at the side of the window, a soft light flooded the room revealing whitewashed walls and dark grey tiles on the floor. Michele told me later that due to the hot summers, it wasn't hygienic to have carpets which, of course, made complete sense. While I relaxed on the well-worn sofa, Michele's mother seated him at the round, heavy wooden table in the middle of the room between herself and her youngest daughter, impatient to know all the news since his last visit. His father intervened occasionally but spent most of the time puffing away on foul-smelling non-filter cigarettes, giving me furtive glances when he thought I wasn't looking.

My ears did their best to acclimatize to the loud volume of Italian conversation and my nostrils tried desperately to cope with the acrid smell of tobacco. In an attempt to quell a coughing fit, I concentrated on my surroundings. The thick, stone walls were painted white, and dark grey tiles made a zigzag pattern on the floor. Tall dark cabinets lined the wall on either side of the door and a small wood-burning stove stood in the corner of the room next to the sofa. A television sat in the opposite corner. I had a niggling feeling that something was missing – but what?

"Would you like a cup of tea?" Michele brought me back to the present.

"Yes, please."

I followed him and his mother into the kitchen where she bustled around, rattling pans in preparation for *spaghetti bolognese*. A large wood-burning stove stood next to a smaller gas stove along the wall and an old-fashioned ceramic sink sporting one tap stood proudly in the corner. I suppose I should have realised from the lone tap that this meant no instant hot water – only cold.

"Come and look at this." Michele called me across to point out a large blue metal container hidden underneath it.

"What is it?" I'd never seen anything like it before.

"It's a *bombola*. We use it for cooking and it contains

fifteen kilos of gas."

"Isn't it dangerous to keep indoors?"

"Yes, *bombolas* 'ave been responsible for serious accidents when faulty valves caused explosions but it doesn't 'appen very often."

That made me very anti- *bombola* from the start. Why couldn't gas be piped to the houses like the rest of Europe?

"They nearly always run out on a Saturday night when the shops are shut – and certainly, there's never a spare one."

While ruminating over the consequences of not having any gas to cook with, I suddenly remembered the tea. I looked furtively over to the worktop for an electric kettle but couldn't see one. Then I saw a teabag floating miserably in a pan of boiling water on the gas stove. Now I'm not one to criticise or give advice where cooking is concerned, but I did get my Badge for Tea Making when I was in the Brownies and even I know that teabags should not be boiled. Nobody offered me any milk, so a few minutes later, sipping my hot water with just the faintest hint of tea, Michele showed me the rest of the house.

"This is the best room which is never used. I don't really know why that is," and he closed the door firmly behind us. I just had time to glimpse a three-piece suite, a small coffee table in the middle and tall sombre glass-paned cabinets full of chalices, plates, dishes, tea and coffee cups before Michele whisked me up the uneven stone stairs. On the landing, a door to the left opened out to the back garden leading to one of the vineyards and to an area where they stored logs for the stoves during the winter months.

"'Ere's the bathroom." He opened a door at the top of the stairs and I breathed a sigh of relief when I saw it consisted of a toilet – a proper one – a bath and a bidet. A tall cylinder for heating the water stood in the corner. A washing machine sat next to the washbasin with a grey pipe hanging over the bath. When in use, that's where the water ran.

"Remember not to 'ave a bath when mum's doing the washing." I shot him a withering look.

"As we 'aven't got constant 'ot water, the water 'eater can be attached to a *bombola* or logs can be burnt."

"How long does the water take to heat up?"

"At least an hour," replied Michele quite cheerfully missing the note of shock-horror in my voice.

"Then again, if it's attached to the *bombola* and it finishes, the water soon runs cold." He shrugged in that loveable way of his, but it somehow didn't have the same effect now as it had in Eastbourne.

"The other problem is that if the water 'eater is lit, everyone decides to 'ave a bath, and if you're last in line, very often you end up with a luke-warm soak."

During the first few weeks, I found myself dreaming about the warm bathroom at home in Poole, with a bath mat on the floor, a shower unit in the bath, and gallons of ready hot water. Relaxing in a bath of soapy bubbles listening to Radio One seemed a lifetime away.

Our bedroom was next to the bathroom and then

more stairs led to the main bedroom on the left where Michele's parents slept and another bedroom on the right which Mara shared with either Anna or Pietro, depending on who happened to be spending the night there. The three bedrooms were all furnished in the same way; two bedside cabinets flanked the beds, a wardrobe stood in one corner and a single chair in the other, presumably used as a clothes horse.

Two single beds had been pushed together in our room and I was just going to ask Michele what his Catholic parents thought about us being together but not married, when his mum appeared in the doorway, and with her son translating, proudly informed me that the mattresses and frames were the same ones that Michele and Pietro had slept on as children. Interesting, was the only non-disparaging word that came to mind.

Last of all, Michele showed me the attic where laundry hung to dry and trunks contained old clothes and bric-a-brac. A scratching noise behind a dusty box made me jump.

"What's that… Aaagh!…" Ignoring my screams, Michele calmly moved the box and I just had time to see a grey streak scuttling across the floor.

"It's only a mouse. You'll frighten it."

"Sorry," I said huffily, trying to stop shaking.

"*E' pronto!*"

Michele's mother's voice echoed from the kitchen and all thoughts of the resident mouse were temporarily forgotten as we joined Mara busily laying the table. As the church bells tolled noon, Carla walked in with a huge bowl of spaghetti and we took our places for the age old ritual of *il pranzo* which is what lunch is called.

"*Buon appetito!*" Michele's dad Alberto said as his wife handed round generous portions of pasta.

Michele's family tried to include me in the conversation but for the moment the language barrier made dialogue impossible. Besides, I had to concentrate on keeping the strings of spaghetti on my fork long enough to put in my mouth. They had a habit of slipping back onto the plate as soon as I lifted the fork. Furthermore, the fact that I drank water instead of wine caused great consternation, judging by the looks being exchanged between Alberto and his wife.

After dishing out second helpings, Mara carried the bowls out to the kitchen before Carla served the next course: steaks with a mixed salad. Having devoured everything, the cheese board appeared. My eyes practically popped out of my head.

"You don't always eat like this, do you?" I asked Michele.

"No, it's usually more but *mamma* didn't 'ave enough time to prepare anything else this morning." Then after a slight pause he added, "We didn't always eat so well when we were children. *Pà* needed all the money 'e earned to build the 'ouse. I remember eating a lot of *polenta* – that's made from corn flour and is very filling, but very boring."

So much for our English lunchtime snacks of baked beans-on-toast or a ham-and-cheese sandwich! An *espresso* brought the meal to an end. I intended helping with the washing-up but Michele and his father invited me to go outside to see the vineyards. Feeling the need to stretch my legs after eating so much, I accepted, not reckoning with the intense heat that once again made me gasp.

Alberto did his best to speak Italian as opposed to the usual village dialect but it made little difference to me; I couldn't understand a word. Michele translated his father's explanation of how he'd planted spindly vines behind the house and nurtured them into their hardy present state. A leafy wooded area enclosed the vineyard.

"We often get deer 'ere," Alberto told me with Michele translating for him. "They damage the vine leaves and are a real menace." He shook his head emphasising the seriousness of it, as he put another cigarette between his lips and lit up.

Opening a gate, we walked down to the track alongside the house, and looking around, I suddenly felt completely awed by the sublime landscape stretching out lazily in front of me. The Alps encircled us clothed in varying shades of luscious greenery, small villages sitting proudly within them and the silvery river snaking down to Lake Como, a light blue blob, just visible in the distance. Surrounded by such natural beauty, with traffic minimal and noise a mere memory, I felt I'd found my very own haven.

On rounding a corner, Alberto proudly showed me an even bigger vineyard. Speaking animatedly and hardly stopping to take a breath, he gave me a lesson in winemaking but the rhythmic sound of his voice lulled me into a comatose state and Michele suggested going home for a *siesta*. I wasn't quite sure what a *siesta* was but I soon found out – I slept soundly all afternoon.

I woke up to hear loud voices from below and recognising Michele's as one of them, I got up and went downstairs to join the family.

"*Ciao!* 'Ere you are at last. This is my sister, Anna, and 'er boyfriend, Filippo and this is Pietro, my brother." Instead of shaking my outstretched hand, each in turn ceremoniously hugged and kissed me on both cheeks. This show of affection unnerved me, yet at the same time made me feel part of the family.

Pietro had arrived home after his shift at the Hotel Villa d'Este in Como where he worked as a receptionist. Fortunately, he spoke English but Anna and Filippo could only smile at me. Anna, an auxiliary nurse in a hospital near Lake Como, came to see her family on her day off when her boyfriend, also a nurse drove her the twenty-minute journey. She wanted to know how we'd met, what I did for a living and what I thought about Italy. Unable to answer for myself, I let my eyes wander over the room while they chatted away to Michele. Again, the niggling feeling that something was missing came back, and then it dawned on me. There were no radiators – just a wood-burning stove. How would we cope with the harsh winters Michele had told me about? I could almost feel the sharp icy blasts of air filling the rooms and making us shiver. For the time being, I decided not to think about it – I already had the summer heat to contend with.

Mara laid the table again and we took our places for

la cena – dinner. After the customary "*Buon appetito*", Carla ladled the soup into our dishes and I had my first plate of *minestra,* followed by an assortment of cold meats, cheese and coffee. Not being able to join in the conversation, I studied my fiancé's family. Michele had already described them to me and I felt as though I knew them.

Papà Alberto, a gaunt, bent man with thinning black hair and a kind disposition, had suffered ill health for most of his married life and the chain-smoking didn't help.

"*Pà* was a great *liscio* dancer when 'e was young," Michele told me before turning to speak to his father, who smiled in my direction, nodding energetically.

"I've just made 'im promise to take you for a spin on the *pista,* that's the dance floor they build, at the next festival where there'll be music and dancing."

"Ok, but what is *liscio*?"

"It's like old-time dancing."

Now retired, Alberto spent his days farming his land. He made his own wine, like most of the people round here, and was proud of its quality. He caught me looking at him and his lined face creased into a smile.

"*Assaggi il vino,*" he coaxed. Michele poured a drop of red wine into my glass.

"Try it – for my *papà*. I know you don't like wine but per'aps you'll like ours."

"I suppose there's no harm in having a sip." The cool ruby liquid slid deliciously down my throat leaving a warm contented feeling inside.

"Well?" Michele asked.

"I like it." I drank some more. "I definitely like it." *Pà* nodded happily and my teetotal days became history.

Funnily enough, my glass always remained full. Somebody topped it up every time I looked away. This seemed to be the pattern for the following meals, too. I must confess it left me glowing and euphoric. I just wanted to laugh. No nostalgia, no thoughts of going back to England. That is, until a strong cup of *espresso* brought me back to my senses. From then on, I decided it would be better to have half a glass at lunchtime and another half at dinner.

A typical Italian *mamma*, Carla's main priority was food and feeding her brood.

"*Mamma's* an excellent cook," Michele had told me in Eastbourne.

I'd groaned at this piece of information; allergic to cookers and recipes and anything else regarding food, my culinary talents still had to emerge.

Each member in turn scrutinized me throughout the *cena*.

"Do you think I've passed the test?" I whispered to Michele later, but he didn't understand the irony of the question.

"I mean, do you think they like me?"

"Why shouldn't they?" That was as good an answer as any for me.

Before going to bed, Michele took me outside to see the view. Silhouetted against an inky black sky with stars shimmering and a full moon, the Alps towered above us and lights winked mischievously high up in their shadows where chalets were homes to farmers and tourists for the hot summer months. I looked hard and long, savouring the smell of pine and the absolute silence broken only by a dog barking in the distance and the unmistakeable sound of crickets hiding in the tall grasses. The magical moment was forgotten later that night, as I tossed and turned, desperately trying to find a cosy spot in the lumpy mattress. I made a conscientious effort to appreciate the historical and sentimental value of what I was lying on, but all I really wanted was to sleep on smooth, modern bedding.

"*Mamma* says that single mattresses are a very sensible idea because you each 'ave your own space," Michele explained the next morning.

I couldn't help thinking that if I'd wanted my own space, I'd have remained single. Personally, I found the two single mattresses very uncomfortable. I always seemed to end up in the middle of them. If and when we ever had a place of our own, I would make sure we had a new and very smooth double mattress.

The following night, I woke up to find something pricking my cheek. Despite the crisp, new pillow-case, the pillow itself wasn't exactly soft and smooth but I managed to fall back to sleep. In the morning I found what looked like a feather on the pillow.

"It's a chicken feather," my mother-in-law-to-be proudly told me with Michele's help. "I stuffed the pillows myself when Pietro and Michele were toddlers."

My new life seemed to be full of reminders of years gone by. I silently added pillows to my list of wants.

3

A Day of Surprises

"Come on, *pà's* going to take us to Cercino." Michele's voice interrupted Mara's attempts to explain something to me regarding her jeans that totally eluded me. I gave her a helpless shrug and smile, despite her patient repetition of the sentence.

"But what was she saying?" I really wanted to know.

"We can ask 'er again later. We're going to Cercino now," Michele grinned.

"How are we going?" It seemed a long way to walk.

"Wait and see…" his cryptic reply made me all the more curious.

I heard a car engine running as we ran down the steps and then I saw it – a cute little stone-coloured Fiat 500 with no less than a convertible roof.

I forgot my initial impression of them being the epitome of impracticality as I crammed into the back seat and Michele climbed in beside his father, who was already puffing on one of his trademark non-filter cigarettes. We jerked down the bumpy track we'd taken three days ago in the taxi – was it really only three days ago? At the bottom, Alberto turned left onto a narrow tarmac road that weaved its way up and round tight corners for about ten minutes.

"Hey, there's no guard rail on this side!" I gawped at a steeply sloping bank of brambles and trees. The engine drowned my voice and then Alberto rattled off a ream of Italian to me, nodding and smiling in the rear mirror.

"It's best to drive in the middle of the road 'ere, just in case…" Very reassuring! I decided that I wouldn't mind if Michele didn't translate everything his father said to me. Crossing my fingers, I hoped we wouldn't pass any other cars and fortunately, we didn't. The houses below us grew smaller and smaller as we spiralled up to Cercino.

"Can you see Morbegno? Down there, on the left." I followed Michele's finger and saw a mass of minute buildings and roads with patches of green, sprawling from the foot of the mountain to the river.

"Colico and Lake Como are over there on your right."

The sun shimmered on the still water in the far distance, giving it a sparkling, romantic aura and I could just make out a few boats glossing around, enjoying the summer day.

We came to a square and his father was carefully negotiating an incredibly narrow passage, when I saw a woman ahead of us. Alberto started tooting his horn.

"*E' mia sorella,*" he explained.

"It's 'is sister, my aunt," Michele translated.

"*Ciao!*" Her face broke into a most disarming smile.

"*Venite a casa, dai!*" and with that she turned on her heels and beckoned us to follow.

31

Five minutes later, I found myself inside a cool, old-fashioned, dimly lit room with a trestle table in the middle and benches on either side. As my eyes became accustomed to the darkness, I saw an elderly man with grey, thinning hair sitting cross-legged almost inside a huge empty fireplace. He jumped up and, pumping my hand, regaled me with a torrent of dialect. Michele tried to translate but soon gave up. His aunt quickly brought out glasses and a bottle of her husband's famous *grappa* inviting me to sit down and taste his brew.

"Be careful," warned Michele. "*Zio* is well-known for 'is *grappa*. One year, it was so potent the effect was like a bomb going off! He was adding 'is secret ingredient as usual, when all of a sudden the contents started bubbling uncontrollably and the barrel shot into the sky like a missile. People saw it for miles around before it disintegrated into thousands of fragments. The explosion sent *zio* flying through the air into their vegetable patch. *Vero, zio*?" His uncle had been following Michele's gestures and nodded at me to confirm his story. Then, turning to Michele, he pointed to his arms and legs.

"*Ah, sì, sì.*" Michele stopped to light a cigarette before continuing.

"*Zio* 'ad pieces of glass embedded in his arms and legs and ended up in hospital but despite being a bit shaken with a few broken ribs and feeling very sore, 'e made 'istory. 'Is *grappa* is sure to give you a boost – you've been warned."

I gingerly sipped the colourless liquid but despite Michele's warning, nothing could have prepared me for the scorching sensation in my throat as the fiery drops caught my breath, making me cough uncontrollably. His aunt and uncle dissolved into fits of laughter nodding their heads, knocking their drinks back as if it were water and gesturing for me to finish the glass. I declined the offer, battling to get my breath, as Michele patted me on the back.

"Come on," he said as Alberto stood up. "We're going to see *pà's* brother who lives just down the road at Siro."

The aunt and uncle shook my hand fervently, inviting me to pop in to see them at any time, ignoring the fact that we couldn't understand each other. Michele and his father suggested walking the short distance and I agreed, thinking it would give me a chance to clear my lungs.

We passed the square again where a few old men sat outside a bar drinking and playing cards and Alberto stopped to exchange pleasantries with them. We went through the narrow passage again and over a narrow, moss-covered old bridge. Trees and shrubs lined the road which soon became a track, and at a junction, I saw a sign announcing Siro. Michele told me that his father had been born there but over the years most families had decided to move to the villages below and only a few remained. The first house belonged to Michele's aunt and uncle. A dog barked furiously as we approached and a number of cats suddenly fled their warm patch of grass in the sun. The door to one of the stables flew open and an older version of Alberto appeared.

"*Ciao!*" Dressed in an overall, he wiped his hands meticulously on a hanky before shaking hands with me.

There followed a quick burst of dialect between the men and then Michele translated for me.

"'Is cows are up the mountain and 'e's come down to make butter and cheese. Do you want to see 'ow it's made?"

Surprisingly enough, I found my dairy lesson really fascinating. Up to then, I'd only ever thought of butter and cheese being delivered to a supermarket and stacked on shelves ready for customers but watching it being processed using age old wooden implements, made me appreciate how much work it involved. Afterwards we went into the house which was almost identical to Michele's parents' house, to meet his wife. They had four children: two boys and two girls about our age.

We readily accepted cold drinks and then I took a back seat as Michele gave a summary of all that had happened since his last visit. Shutting myself off from the excited hum of conversation, I let my mind wander over the family members I'd met so far, their appearances and behaviour, their houses, their jobs. I'd come to a farming area where the people were rough and ready. I just hoped I'd fit in. Feeling Michele's eyes on mine, I realised he'd asked me a question.

"*Zia* wanted to know if you'd like to see the 'ouse while *pà* and *zio* talk about the vines." I said I'd love to and Michele told me that in its original state, the house had been divided between several family members.

"Three emigrated to California in the early 1900s because so many families were poor at the turn of the century and a number of people chose a new life in

America and Australia." Michele listened to his aunt before continuing. "The relatives never returned to Siro. They married and made their 'ome there and communicated by letters until they died." *Zia* shook her head sadly at the thought of her uncles and aunt.

Walking out into the back garden, *zia* pointed to the right-hand part of the house.

"This is where *zia* used to live," Michele lit up another cigarette and inhaled slowly. "And this is the room where an American soldier 'id during the Second World War and later escaped over the border to Switzerland. *Zia* said she remembers going to feed the chickens and seeing a shadow be'ind the wall. When she screamed, a young man in uniform came out, asking 'er to be quiet. She couldn't understand what 'e was saying but it was obvious that 'e was very cold, 'ungry, frightened and exhausted." Michele stopped while *zia* continued her story, then he translated for me.

"When she realised that 'e wasn't a dangerous criminal, she invited 'im to follow her into the 'ouse and gave 'im something to eat and drink. Her brothers and sisters, who lived with 'er, recognised 'is uniform as being American and some'ow they managed to make themselves understood."

Walking inside the room, now used as a cellar, I could almost feel the tension and fear in the damp air ingrained in the four walls all those years ago. I closed my eyes, imagining the young American soldier battling for survival in a foreign country, alone and desperate, unable to believe his luck on finding this Italian family who wanted to help him. Despite the heat outside, I shivered. Michele went on to explain the horrors of the war when families became divided because one chose to follow fascism and Mussolini, while the others became partisans.

"In this area, most people were partisans and groups risked their lives to take soldiers across the mountains to freedom in Switzerland. *Zia* said that the soldier stayed with them until one of these organizations managed to get the necessary papers for 'im before 'is escape to neutral territory." Michele paused as *zia* whispered something in his ear, as though she was afraid she could be overheard. Softly spoken at the best of times, Michele had to lean forward to hear what *zia* was saying.

"Ah, *zia* said that one evening, a fascist party came to the 'ouse to ask if they'd seen an American soldier. Not 'appy with their answer: 'No, no!', the fascists, dressed in their regulation, black uniforms and their rifles ready to shoot, decided to search the 'ouse and barns. The family could only pray that the youth 'ad the presence of mind to outwit them. An hour later, the fascists left, convinced that the American was still somewhere around. In fact, 'e'd 'idden be'ind sacks of potatoes and…"

This impromptu history lesson was interrupted by Alberto and his brother joining us.

"Why did you stop talking so suddenly?" I asked Michele.

"They both served in the Second World War and were prisoners of war in Germany. They were badly treated and that's mainly the cause of their bad 'ealth. Both of them 'ate talking about it. Maybe one day *pà* will tell you about 'is experiences, but not now."

"Ok, but did the American soldier escape to Switzerland?" I had to know.

Michele whispered something to *zia* before nodding to me.

"Yes, 'e did."

Just as we were saying goodbye, Michele's cousins, Remo and Gianni arrived. They were builders and had finished work early – apparently all the cement had been used up and there was no sense in making more half an hour before downing tools. Remo told Michele that their sister, Daniela, was working in Switzerland and if we wanted to, we were very welcome to accompany him the next time he went to see her. We accepted there and then.

Back in Piussogno, I asked Michele if I could iron a few items. Although we'd emptied our suitcases as soon as we'd arrived, our clothes were nevertheless creased and I wanted to make a good impression. I imagined every householder owned an ironing board but this, too, was missing, along with electric kettles, toasters and non-stick pans.

"How can I iron my clothes and your shirts?" I enquired. With Michele translating, Carla told me to put a cloth on the small kitchen table and use that. So be it, who was I to quibble?

"Oops, I keep running out of table when it comes to ironing my long skirts." I laughed.

The novelty soon wore off as it took me twice as long to iron out the creases. Just as I began tackling Michele's shirts, Carla walked into the kitchen and more by gesticulating than verbally, told me that I hadn't ironed Michele's sleeves properly. Feeling frustrated and uncomfortably hot, I found it impossible to appreciate her help at that precise moment and maybe it was just as well the language barrier existed.

"Come on," Michele said, no doubt sensing the tension. "Let's go for a walk."

In record time, I put everything away and joined him before he changed his mind. Walking hand-in-hand up to the vineyard, we bumped into more of Michele's innumerable relatives. It seemed that every other person in the village was related to him.

"This is *zio*… and *zia*… " I forgot their unpronounceable names instantly.

No one, it seemed, moved away from their place of birth or if they did, it was never further than the next village. I began to understand why people thought I was mad to have left my hometown and settle in a foreign country, 1,649 km away.

"'E's *pa's* younger brother and that's their 'ouse over there." Michele translated for his uncle, who in turn, indicated his home with the largest pair of hands I'd ever seen. I was still staring at them when he started talking. Words tumbled over each other in quick succession and I wondered when a sentence stopped and another began.

"*Zia*," Michele explained, "looks after their granddaughter while their eldest daughter, Lella, who's

38

your age, works in a local factory. And these are their nine year-old twins, the youngest members of the family."

Still fascinated with his uncle's hands and the way he gesticulated with them as he spoke, without thinking I said: "Hello!" to Tina and Gino. Huge, brown eyes stared up at me and their mouths dropped open as they both regarded me in awe, convinced I'd come from another planet.

"Non sa parlare Italiano? E' impossibile - tutti sanno l'Italiano!"

Michele translated for me, imitating their incredulity: "What, she can't speak Italian? It's impossible – everyone knows Italian!" Hearing their big cousin speak English they started giggling. Then, after scrutinising me from head to toe, they plucked up enough courage to touch my arm to see if I was real. Satisfied that I wasn't some kind of android, they smiled at each other and with a nod in our direction, grabbed their two year-old niece's chubby hands and ran off towards the house.

"Bambini!" said *zia*, shaking her head in mock despair.

*

That evening after dinner, I asked Michele if I could ring mum to let her know we'd arrived safely and everything was fine. Funnily enough, another essential commodity missing from houses in Piussogno was a telephone. I didn't want to appear pessimistic or dramatic but a phone, to me, was a dire necessity.

"There's a public phone at the bar," he told me. "It's the one I used to ring when I was working in Germany, Switzerland and England. I'd ring the bar and ask Alda to tell *mamma* that I'd call again the following day, and she would go at the arranged time. That's 'ow I've always kept in touch with my family." He thought nothing of it.

"Pietro told me that now it is possible to ring from 'ere, though but you can't dial directly to England. You 'ave to ring the telephone exchange in Rome, book the call to Poole, then wait an hour or more to be put through. On the other 'and," Michele paused dramatically, "we could drive to Switzerland, it only takes between forty-five minutes to an hour to get to the border, and, in the first bar we come to, you could ring your mum without any problem."

Of course, a minor obstacle was the lack of a car and no way could we tootle to Heidi country in Michele's father's bubble car. We would have to rely on someone to take us. Remo's name came to mind, and although I wouldn't be alone with Michele, it would still be a treat. It also meant we had the chance to buy Swiss chocolate and jars of Nescafé.

The following morning, gloomy dark clouds predicted a storm and for some unknown reason, I felt uneasy. I put it down to the sultry weather and the fact that the slightest clap of thunder reduced me to a nervous tremble, but when Pietro came home from his night shift, one look at his face confirmed my worst fears. Michele and I had planned to work at the hotel Villa d'Este in

Como during the summer to earn some money but Pietro solemnly told us that whereas Michele's job was still open for him – mine was not – and, even worse, he had to start work the following day. It took a moment for me to digest this last piece of information. It suddenly dawned on me that I would have to stay with my future in-laws all on my own.

Fighting back hot salty tears as I said goodbye to Michele wasn't easy, especially as I wouldn't see him again for a week until his first day off. I tried to think positively, however. At least I could really find out for myself whether I wanted to spend the rest of my life here or not.

"I'll only be gone a week," Michele tried to reassure me.

"A week's a long time," the words popped out before I knew it.

"Look, if you need anything just ask Pietro. I've got to go now. See you on Friday." I grabbed his arm and gave him one last kiss before he climbed into the car.

Waving a little too enthusiastically, I stamped a wide smile on my face, telling myself I'd see him every weekend and the time apart would surely fly by. I hadn't realised how much I'd relied on Michele to translate for me until then. Now it was all up to me.

4

Home Alone

I had no job, no friends, and no one to confide in. For the first time in my life I was totally alone. It was a real test of character, especially as I'm not the quietest of people, but it was certainly a lesson in listening as well as in observing another culture.

Michele's mum wanted to know what I was good at – cooking, sewing, gardening? Unfortunately, the answer was none of the above, but Michele told her I could play the piano, paint with oils and water colours, and teach primary children, as well as English to foreign students. Unsurprisingly, my curriculum vitae meant nothing to Carla so she decided that I should help with the housework instead of working in the kitchen or in the vineyards. After breakfast, I began my daily chores of sweeping the tiles – I'd have given anything for a hoover – polishing the furniture and lastly, washing the floors. To do the latter, I had to use a bucket of cold water, cloth and scrubbing brush on a long handle. Squeezy mops and rubber gloves still had to make their debut at No. 18, Via Fiesso.

"What exactly am I doing here?" I asked myself on

more than one occasion, immersing the dirty cloth in the bucket and wringing the water out of it while my well-manicured hands became red and blotchy.

Having trained to be a teacher, and growing up wanting only to teach, I found my new job as a cleaner more than tedious. The senior schools I had contacted regarding teaching English had replied positively – what they had failed to say was that I had to take a degree in an Italian university first. My education had spanned seventeen years in the U.K. and I had no inclination to start studying again in Italy. I felt torn between my life-long dream of a teaching career and wanting to be with Michele. For the time being, I resigned myself to the role of academic cleaner.

Unlike the usual weekly shopping we did at the nearest supermarket in Poole, here families bought their food on a daily basis and so I opted to accompany Mara to the shop for two reasons: firstly, in the hope of picking up new vocabulary and whiling away the hours until noon and secondly, I didn't feel ready to stay alone with Carla because she had a habit of talking to herself as she prepared the meals and I never really understood whether she was rehearsing future conversations or repeating the menu of the day. Whatever it was, to my ears her tone didn't encourage idle chatter.

"It's only 'er manner," Michele assured me when I confessed my uneasiness within the confines of our bedroom one weekend. "Don't worry."

I tried not to. Then I remembered my radio. Music has always been an intrinsic part of my life and, desperate to listen to anything other than a silence broken only by the sloshing of water as I rinsed the cloth before washing the floor, I brought my transistor down from the bedroom and tuned into the first radio station I found, even though I did not understand a word. I'm an ardent fan of Cliff Richard, but this was better than nothing.

"Music is music in any language and I can hum," I told myself, as I dusted the cabinets. Whether or not Carla appreciated the modern impromptus that filled the house, I'll never know.

*

I tried gesticulating and miming when no one understood my desperate attempts to put a coherent sentence together but sometimes even that didn't work. I mean, how on earth did I explain that a couple of turkeys had suddenly materialised from nowhere and chased me almost all the way home? I'd gone to the shop that morning with Mara and when she met her friend, I walked on ahead never thinking for one moment that I would be attacked by the psycho-wildlife of Piussogno. My shrieks for help as I dodged the gobbling fowls fell on deaf ears as several locals found the scene more than amusing, nodding and grinning, revealing few teeth and a great amount of gums. Back home, I found Carla in the kitchen, cooking as usual. She stopped and stared at my flushed face as I practically fell through the door.

"*Ciao,*" I could still feel my heart thudding as I looked up 'turkey' in the dictionary.

"*Tacchino correre me.*" I made running movements with my fingers, then enacted my dilemma with the ferocious birds, but Carla missed the message in the role play, probably because with arms splayed and flapping wildly, while running around the table, I most likely resembled someone who needed help with more than the language. At the end of my exhibition she stared at me then with hands on her hips she said:

"*Non tacchino per pranzo, pasta.*" And promptly went back to preparing lunch. Guessing that pasta would be served shortly and not turkey, I set about laying the table.

*

One noticeable item missing from the fridge was a bottle of milk. In its place, Michele had shown me a jug full of frothy fresh milk which had to be boiled before drinking and told me that every evening at 6 pm, armed with a metal cylindrical container with a lid, Mara walked to the local dairy in Piussogno to buy it. I was curious to know what the dairy was like and where it was, and Michele suggested I went with her. When Mara stopped outside what looked like an old stable, I recalled that we always passed it on our way to do the shopping. Walking inside, I saw a man with a discoloured brown apron tied over corduroy trousers and a well-worn shirt with the sleeves rolled up, using weighing equipment that I was sure I had seen in the Victorian section of Poole Museum. The dairyman carefully ladled the milk from huge silver containers into the customer's small metal one before weighing it on the old fashioned scales and giving the price. Coins deftly passed between them before the money disappeared into the folds of the apron and the next tin was handed over.

One evening, Mara couldn't go to fetch the milk, so I volunteered. It didn't occur to me that I wouldn't understand if anyone spoke to me or no one would understand me. The dairyman became very animated when he heard the word: *inglesina* (English girl) being repeated by the waiting customers. As I handed over the container, I got the surprise of my life.

"'Ello. What are you doing 'ere, then?" I looked at him blankly. At first it didn't register, but then I realised that he was actually talking to me in my native tongue. He had lived in Australia for some years. We chatted for quite a while, completely oblivious to the queue forming behind me in the small room. I was so excited to find someone else who spoke English, I forgot to pay and he had to run outside after me and call me back. I felt awful and apologised profusely.

Now and again, I accompanied Mara to get the milk, enjoying a quick chat in English. It was fine when the weather was good, but when there was a summer storm with torrential rain, lightning zigzagging across the sky followed by a slow menacing rumble echoing around the mountains, it was a different matter. I didn't exactly crave fresh milk anyway if it had to be heated before drinking. I resigned myself to the fact that if milkmen didn't have a role in Italian life then I'd have to adapt to drinking milk from cartons. I missed my English chats but no way did I miss enduring the elements in all weathers just for a litre of milk.

"Why are there so few young people here in Piussogno?" On my walks, I hadn't met too many teenagers.

"Quite a few work away in 'otels and only come 'ome for special occasions and 'olidays. Others have jobs in Switzerland," Michele explained. "Don't forget that I went to work in a 'otel in Milan when I was sixteen. I came back now and again but if you think about it, I've been away for seven years." That accounted for the ever-present older population. The couples I'd met with toddlers were even younger than me and Michele explained that quite a lot were shotgun weddings. The children were invariably brought up by the grandparents.

"Doesn't the pill exist here?" Silly question, and, in fact, Michele didn't answer.

*

To say I suffered from mood swings would be an understatement. Without Michele, I felt lost, angry and frustrated, wondering what I was doing in this age-old village. Although we were living in the seventies, it was as if time had frozen in an ever-distant past. There was no cinema, no theatre, no sports centre, no library. In fact, Piussogno didn't exactly have a lot going for it and the inhabitants, although friendly enough, were used to working the land and men and women alike spent hours digging, planting and pruning.

"Do you like it here?" They'd ask me in dialect, blatantly eyeing me up and down, nodding. I found it off-putting, to put it mildly. Having been brought up with the British view that staring is very rude, their brazen scrutiny left me at a loss for words.

"It's only their way of making you feel at 'ome." Michele always had a feasible answer.

"Well, maybe they could stop looking at me as if I've got two heads, then."

The villagers all had the same brown, leathery faces – I doubt if many of the women had ever used make-up or moisturiser – and they sported well-worn and practical clothes, all except for their clogs, that is.

"*Questi sono per te*," Mara handed me a plastic bag a couple of weeks after our arrival.

"*Grazie*," I opened it gingerly and discovered a pair of clogs, more or less my size. She said something to Pietro who then translated for me.

"*Mamma* says you can't keep wearing your nice shoes and sandals because you'll ruin them and Mara 'ad these spare ones which should fit. She bought them from a place called *Premana*, a mountain village in Valsassina above Lecco. It's famous for making knives, scissors and wooden clogs." I thanked her again and tried on the new wooden clogs, laughing inadvertently as I found it virtually impossible to keep them on just sitting down, let alone walking in them.

"Help!" I cried as I took three steps before tripping over. How come I found it so difficult? Not to be outdone by a pair of clogs, I slipped them on again, inhaled deeply and walked towards the gate. That's what I intended doing, but they seemed to have a will of their own and I found myself sprawled on the ground without realising what had happened.

"Ouch, that hurt!" This time I managed to graze my knee. "Um, maybe it's better if I go on wearing my *nice* shoes and sandals after all." I relegated the clogs to the bedroom – and there they stayed.

The women, I noticed, never went far without a headscarf – even indoors – or the compulsory overall. But, although determined to adapt as best I could, I had no intention of changing my English look. Walking around in my flowing skirts, cheesecloth shirts and open sandals, with my face made up with Max Factor's natural look, I suppose I stood out like a sunflower in a bunch of daisies.

Having a lot of time on my hands didn't help. I missed Michele terribly and I couldn't help asking myself if I'd done the right thing by following him to his hometown. In the 1970s, the mentality in the Valtellina was still very male-orientated and most women stayed at home looking after the children. The majority of the men expected ashtrays to materialise on their own and to help lay the table or do the washing-up were initiatives that still had to be discovered. As yet, Michele hadn't undergone a complete metamorphosis and I sincerely hoped he wouldn't. At times the cultural differences seemed insuperable. Then I'd hear the young cousins calling me to join them on one of their expeditions into the woods behind the vineyards to look for a bird's nest and their smiling faces, often smudged with Nutella from the roll they'd be sharing, made me laugh and forget all the dark thoughts. Sometimes it would be me who made them laugh, though. A stream flowed not far from the side of the house and to avoid taking the longer path down to the road to the square, Mara suggested we take the shortcut which involved jumping across the rocks jutting out of the water. She made light work of it. I, on the other hand, being less nimble, had to negotiate the steps to the other side. It soon became a source of amusement to her and her cousins to watch me teeter across.

"Dai, dai! Ce la fai." Mara's words of encouragement didn't help.

I jealously witnessed her aunt literally leap across despite her age and bulk and from then on I vowed to do likewise… and I did, almost. I had a knack of missing my footing on the last stone and ending up in the cool water. Despite talk of impending drought, the stream never dried up completely, ensuring wet sandals for me each time.

Mara took after her father and Michele both physically and in temperament. She had long, black hair and dark brown eyes that reflected her mood. At 13, she couldn't wait to finish middle school, so that she could go to Morbegno, the nearest town, where she would begin her apprenticeship at a hairdresser's. Her ready smile and bubbly laugh encouraged me in moments of despair when I found communication to be hopelessly beyond my comprehension. I genuinely believed the language barrier to be a temporary obstacle but as the days became weeks and I still couldn't make myself understood, disillusionment and impatience set in. Mara did her best to teach me words and phrases.

"*Ripeti: ho fame.*" She rubbed her tummy to show she was hungry.

"*Ho fame,*" I repeated. She clapped her hands then gestured encouragingly to show me that I was getting there.

She followed me everywhere, and despite her rule of not leaving the house during the hottest hours of the day, she joined me on my walks around the village, in my case to burn the calories – the plates of pasta were taking their toll and my jeans had become more than figure-hugging.

"*Non è un problema,*" Mara had smiled, as I tried desperately to keep the bulging flesh inside the jeans and do the zip up.

"Not a problem, it's a nightmare! How am I going to lose weight before Michele comes home again?" I prodded the offending ring of surplus skin that had slowly grown over the last three weeks.

Using sign language, Mara told me to lie on the bed while she took out a metal coat hanger from the wardrobe. Trying not to look too worried as she climbed onto the bed behind me, I watched her put the curved metal piece into the hole in the zip.

"*Pronta?*" she asked. As ready as I'd ever be, I nodded. Flexing her muscles, she pulled as hard as she could and - *zaaap*! The zip closed miraculously.

"*Ecco, fatto,*" She helped me to my feet and I thankfully realised I could just about stand up and breathe at the same time. Patting my now very flat belly, I decided that I definitely needed more exercise. The coat hanger would only be used again in dire circumstances. I also learnt two more words: *ecco, fatto* – meaning: that's done. I was making progress.

"Come on," I gestured to Mara, "it's time for a walk."

She nodded and five minutes later, ignoring the fierce summer temperatures, we made our way to the village square.

Suddenly, I thought I heard the sound of horses' hooves. I stopped to listen, unsure as to whether the sun and heat were finally getting to me.

"*Sì, sì. E' un cavallo,*" said Mara, as if she had read my mind.

Sure enough, an old horse came plodding into view, guided by reins firmly held by the elderly farmer sitting on the cart.

"*Bondì!*" he shouted the usual salute in dialect to us, as he went by. Newly cut hay spilled over the sides of the cart and left a trail as it lurched over the cobbled stones.

We both replied with: "*Salve.*" I tried, without much success not to stare open-mouthed.

"I don't believe it – a horse and cart being used for transport in the twentieth century."

Surprisingly enough, after that encounter, I saw several carts being pulled by horses, not only around the village but also on the roads, even though such an attraction seemed more appropriate as entertainment at a fete, a pageant or a festival than on a main road, dangerously defying the speed and power of high tech machinery, better known as cars. Needless to say, traffic was relatively light in the seventies in our area. Several pensioners in the village still used this method to carry tree trunks and hay from their fields back to their barns, a reminder of years gone by when it was their sole means of conveyance. Living in houses higher up the mountain, it was often the only way to negotiate the rough paths and tracks.

"Why should we change our way of life? Cars pollute the air, they cause accidents, they are expensive to run, and they are prone to breaking down. Not so with a mule, a horse or a donkey. They are dependable, healthy for the environment, and a trusted friend and companion. And do they ever moan or complain? No, no, no!" Their mantra never changed. Sometimes I'd see entire families sitting on the back of the cart, armed with scythes and rakes, on their way to cut the hay in a field.

One man who went everywhere with his mule and cart was known as *il cieco*, the blind man. No one would have realised from his manner that he couldn't see. He walked with the aid of a stick but still managed to guide his cart and mule along the road.

"I'm sure he can see," I argued with Michele "or perhaps he has developed an acute sixth sense."

"Whoa!" he'd cry and the mule would plod slowly along the side of the road, allowing plenty of room for the car to overtake. He could tell if someone was walking towards him. On one occasion, I saw him ambling along, leading his mule this time. I deliberately slowed my steps and tried to tread as quietly as possible. He still greeted me with a jovial "*Buongiorno*" a good ten metres before I reached him. He and his wife lived in a house in the village square next to Michele's aunt and uncle. He became a familiar sight, going backwards and forwards, his cart loaded with long trunks of wood which had to be chopped into logs for the wood-burning stove, ready for the cold winter months ahead.

"When I was at primary school," Michele told me, "My friends used to play jokes on Negri. That's the blind man's name. As 'e walked by the wall near the school on 'is way to the bar, they could 'ear the tap, tap, tap his stick made and they would take it in turns to lean over and grab 'is 'at. Once, as the boy lifted 'is 'at, Negri gave him a sharp rap on the 'ead with the stick. 'ow did Negri know 'e was in that exact spot? 'ow did he manage to 'it the boy? It was just incredible. Like you, we decided 'e must be able to see after all and from that day on, the jokes stopped – just in case."

Although it worried me to find myself in a time warp, it also intrigued me to see these elderly villagers who shunned modern sources of transport, sitting proudly on their carts, gnarled fingers wrapped around the reins, clucking to their horses.

*

Michele came home every Friday and I couldn't wait to tell him what I'd learnt or done during his absence. Living with his family meant they all wanted to speak to him, too, and I had to wait my turn. Patience, I regret to admit, is not one of my virtues, so I had to work out a plan to have time alone with my fiancé. After listening to him discussing all-important matters with his parents and brother and sister, I feigned an urgent need to go for a walk.

"Is everything all right?" he asked, tentatively.

"Yes and no. I just wanted you to myself." I kissed him lightly on the lips.

Strolling along, hand-in-hand, it dawned on me that nearly all the houses in the village were two-storey buildings.

"How come all the houses are so big? There aren't any bungalows at all."

Michele smiled before answering.

"Whereas young people in England move into flats of their own as soon as they can, 'ere, no one moves away from 'ome and when the son finally decides to marry, they just move into the flat upstairs." He waited for my reaction and he wasn't disappointed. As the significance of having two storeys sunk in, my mouth dropped open. The grooms expected the young brides to leave their family home to move into a flat above their in-laws, confirming the theory that Italian men found it practically impossible to break away from their *mamma*. There and then, it dawned on me that Michele was definitely a mummy's boy, despite his hot denial.

"I see." I replied, striding ahead of him. "Does this mean that we'll stay with your parents when we're married and I'll have to wait on you like a lackey?

"What are you talking about?"

"I mean, what's wrong with a woman having a vocation other than that of wife and mother? This is the twentieth century, for goodness sake."

"What do you mean? Why are you so angry?" I felt Michele's eyes boring into me, probably wondering who this fractious person was, but I'd had enough. I hadn't seen him for a week and then I could only have him all to myself if we went for a walk because there was always someone vying for his attention in the house.

"Angry? Me? Do you realise I gave up my career to follow you and we're not even together? I think I'm entitled to be somewhat *angry*." My voice hung shrilly in the air. We were having our first real row since we'd arrived in Italy. A couple of farmers stopped raking hay into a stable between two houses and leaned on their forks, openly enjoying our spat. This would liven up conversation during their evening meal.

"You see, we can't even row in private!" I pointed to our audience.

Wanting to avoid a scene, Michele tried to pacify me:

"Look, when we're in our own flat above *mamma* and *pà*…"

"What? If you think we're going to live with them, you can think again." This was going from bad to worse and Michele was due back in Como the following day. Unfamiliar tears tried desperately to seep out but I choked them back. His hurt look made me feel guilty.

"Sorry." I took his hand in mine. "It's just that I'm not used to sharing you with everyone. I didn't think I'd miss you so much, either. Sometimes it's awful being here by

56

myself and not knowing the language doesn't help. I thought I'd pick it up really quickly but I still can't have a conversation with anyone." Burying my head in his neck, the tears gushed out together with the repressed feelings of insecurity and utter dejection. He wrapped his arms around me and seeing that the quarrel had ended, the farmers stubbed out their cigarettes and reluctantly went back to work.

"It'll be all right, you'll see." He whispered into my hair.

"I hope so," I whispered back.

5

Back to School

'What an incredible experience,' I thought to myself, 'to remain silent and listen to a number of Italians all talking together at the same time.'

Having been brought up to wait until the speaker had finished before replying, and never to raise one's voice, the Baronas fascinated me by the way that they could accommodate six different conversations simultaneously. Sigmund Freud would have been proud of them.

The fact that they spoke dialect and not Italian didn't help matters. Each village, town and city had its very own, very different dialect. This revelation, I admit, did squash my initial reaction that learning the language would be a cinch.

"How am I ever going to learn Italian?"

"Oh, you'll learn," Michele said before going back to his ever-present sports paper.

Unfortunately, the small pocket English/Italian dictionary that Michele had used in Eastbourne didn't help me at all because it didn't contain the words used in dialect. My accent proved another source of amusement. I suppose I tried to speak Italian with a BBC accent, instead of pronouncing the words phonetically and exaggerating the vowels.

"*Weilà. Come sta?*" The villagers invariably shouted out to me.

"They want to know 'ow you are," Michele explained but due to the language barrier, many assumed that raising their voices would help my understanding – if only. It was a challenge but I still thought I'd master the Italian language quickly and easily.

Michele's young cousins took me around Piussogno most days and they taught me quite a lot. To them it was a game and I wasn't afraid of making mistakes – we just laughed. They set about teaching me a few words and delighted in getting me to repeat phrases.

"*Prova a dire: ' buongiorno'*," they coaxed.

"*Buongiono*," I repeated.

"*Ma, no!*" they fell about laughing. "Buongiorno, *devi pronunciare la* **erre.**"

"Ok. *Buongiorno.*"

"*Brava, brava, brava!*"

They were excellent teachers but unfortunately, not good enough to make me fluent.

One afternoon, I tried to impress them with a phrase I had heard Pietro use but instead of looking at me with renewed respect as I'd hoped, they stopped in their tracks, glancing furtively around to see if anyone else had heard.

"Nooo!" they chorused.

I wondered what I had said and couldn't wait to ask Michele.

"Adults can use that particular expression but not children," he explained later.

I also had a habit of saying '*Ciao'* to everyone I met, instead of using the more formal *Buongiorno*.

"*Non puoi dire 'Ciao' a quella signora. Devi dire 'Buongiorno'!*" The children would pretend to tell me off before dissolving into fits of giggles.

The language barrier became even more pronounced with Michele in Como. Pietro worked as night porter in the same hotel and slept for most of the day when he came home. At least I could ask him for help if I really got stuck. With only a thirteen-month age gap between them, Michele and Pietro were very close as brothers, even working together abroad in hotels, and both could speak four languages. But, unlike Michele, Pietro was more reserved. Too much in awe of my future brother-in-law and too proud to admit defeat, I decided I had to overcome this obstacle by myself. Flicking through the English/Italian dictionary, I tried to talk to Carla as she clattered around the kitchen.

"*Volere aiutare. Sì?*"

She stopped her banging and looked at me blankly.

"Um, *potere fare?*" I tried again, wishing I'd studied Latin at school, but shaking her head, she paused for a second then went back to her cooking, saying something only she could understand.

"Okay, how about this: *come fare?*" Carla turned and

shrugged her shoulders. Frustration simmered inside me like a volcano about to erupt. The sooner I learnt to speak the language, the better.

"*No, no, no!*" I gave a sigh of relief as Mara appeared in the doorway, laughing.

"Oh, *ciao*. Listen, how do I say, 'Can I help you?' um, *potere aiutare?*" She nodded, understanding what I meant and turned to her mother, presumably repeating what I wanted to say. After an exchange of words, Carla looked at me for a long moment, then opened a drawer and took out a duster, indicating the furniture. I promptly took the cloth and began polishing.

When Mara and I went shopping, I bought a newspaper, believing that translating it would help me learn the language. After three days, I still hadn't finished translating half of the first page.

I had a brain wave, I could watch television. At least I'd be listening to Italian and not dialect.

Another bitter lesson in failure; it took two days to work out how to say 'where' in Italian. No matter how hard I tried to understand, I often felt left out when conversation with the family proved beyond me. Fed up and bored at not being able to join in, I realised I couldn't learn the language by myself. I needed help – professional help. The following weekend when Michele arrived home, instead of reeling off what I'd done during his absence, I had a request: "Do you know anyone who could teach me Italian as soon as possible?" He picked up on the sheer desperation in my voice.

"Give me a minute." He disappeared before I could

answer. Just for a change, I joined his cousins for a walk to the square but they sensed my pensive mood and spoke together more quietly than usual, each glancing at me when they thought I wasn't looking.

"I've spoken to Luisa and she says she'll be only too 'appy to teach you Italian," Michele announced later that evening.

"Who's Luisa?" I asked. Her name hadn't been mentioned before.

"She's Adriano's wife and they live in the square. She teaches at the pre-school in Traona. She said you can start lessons tomorrow afternoon, if you like."

"If I like? That's fantastic!"

At last someone could help me get over the language barrier. That night I went to bed happy. I naturally presumed that Italian grammar would be similar to English and as I had already taught English to foreign students, I felt confident I'd make an able pupil.

At the appointed hour I arrived at her house armed with an exercise book, a pencil case, my dictionary and lots of enthusiasm. Luisa smiled warmly as she opened the door and I estimated she was about five years older than me.

"*Ciao, sono Luisa. Vieni, vieni.*" With the introductions over, I followed her into the lounge and the lesson began. After half an hour, my initial high spirits started to fade. I had no idea Italian grammar was so complicated and difficult. The tenses were never-ending and no matter how hard I tried, I found myself drowning in a sea of unintelligible verbs. At that point, I wondered whether it would be better to learn dialect instead. Still, my teacher didn't intend giving up on me. With an encouraging smile and a pat on the arm, she said: "*Scrivi di nuovo*," gesturing for me to rewrite the main tenses, then: "*Ripeti ancora*," from her actions, I gathered I had to repeat them orally. Several were very difficult to pronounce and Luisa made me repeat them over and over again.

"Do I really need to practise these verbs or do you just like hearing my English interpretation of them?" I asked, smiling.

Obviously not understanding a word I'd said, Luisa shook her head, grinning: "*Dai, italiano, soltanto italiano*." I gathered I had to speak Italian, only Italian.

"Okay," at least that was international.

"Okay," she echoed, and my lesson continued.

"*Brava, brava*," she said cheerfully when I finally got it right. Then, looking at her watch, she let out a shriek.

"*Ma, no, sono le 5. E' ora del tè!*" And with that, Luisa jumped up and put a saucepan of water on the gas stove to boil, then her head disappeared inside a cabinet. A lot of clinking and clattering followed before she jubilantly produced a squashed Twinings tea bag.

"Okay?" she asked, tentatively.

"Okay." I smiled and she visibly relaxed.

We cleared the books away and made space for the cups and saucers and a huge plate of mouth-watering assorted biscuits. This became a daily pattern; at precisely 5pm, we stopped for a cup of tea. It's a foregone conclusion – for Italians – that everywhere in

England, we drink tea at that enchanted hour. No matter how hard I tried to explain that tea could be consumed at any hour, she never offered me a cup at any other time.

I spent the first couple of weeks learning verbs: present, past, future, conditional, imperative. You name it I studied it. I took my lessons seriously and did my homework conscientiously. I had no means of cheating or copying.

"But when will I learn to speak fluently?" I asked her in exceedingly bad Italian.

"*Pazienza, pazienza!*" She smiled, I groaned.

I became more and more frustrated and disillusioned.

"If I concentrate, I can understand what's being said to me. The problem is replying coherently," I whinged to Michele one Friday evening. "And don't say I need to be patient..."

"All right, I won't." That really wound me up.

"It's awful not being able to speak."

"I bet it is," he laughed. "It's certainly a change for you to be quiet. In Eastbourne you were like a 'uman radio at times, only I couldn't turn you off."

"Thanks." I tried to hit him with a cushion but he managed to dodge.

My lessons continued every afternoon, finishing with the ritual of tea and biscuits. No wonder my waistline grew and the hanger ritual had to be used again on several occasions when I wanted to wear my jeans. Then, just as I prepared to accept the fact that my slim-line body would become a mere memory, lesson eleven brought euphoria. I learnt to say I had eaten enough and didn't want anymore. I practised the phrase over and over to perfect my accent, hoping to impress the family. I didn't have to wait long before the opportunity presented itself one lunchtime. Just as Carla tried ladling more pasta onto my plate, I interrupted her with a sweet smile: "*Sono sazia, non ne voglio più, grazie.*"

Three pairs of eyes bored into mine and then they looked at Carla as she put the pasta on her own plate. The awkward silence that followed crushed my ego and I knew that although I'd saved my thickening waistline, I'd lost points in Carla's eyes. Too late, I wished that I hadn't thought of making an impact during lunch – food was far too important for that. From now on, I would keep my newly acquired oral skills to myself or at least, for occasions other than mealtimes.

Each day I tried to memorise five words chosen at random from my dictionary, a sure way of enriching my vocabulary. I continued buying a newspaper and gradually, more and more words became familiar. I started watching the news and felt so excited when I managed to get the gist of what the reader was saying.

"Guess what I learnt today?" I told Michele, reciting the verbs and conjugations.

"Hmm," he replied and went back to reading the sports page. I gathered that Italian grammar wasn't his favourite subject. For once we had the lounge to ourselves so I decided on another tactic to attract his attention. Luisa had taught me a special phrase for Michele which I'd been saving for the right moment to surprise him.

"*Amore, ti voglio bene*," I breathed into his ear – and it worked. His eyes spoke volumes as the paper fell to the floor and his lips brushed mine in a kiss that beat any scene from a film.

"*Brava, brava!* I love you, too," he murmured, pulling me closer. The moment lasted only a few seconds before Mara burst into the room. The joys of living all together in one household were endless. Jumping apart as if we'd been stung by a laser gun, Michele retrieved his paper and I picked up my Italian textbook and continued studying as demurely as possible.

A few days later, I met Michele's aunt and amazed her by putting a sentence together coherently. Sheer elation shot through my body at being given an answer instead of a blank stare. The fact that the reply wasn't completely comprehensible to me didn't matter – I was making progress.

Michele's family made a point of correcting my pronunciation. I had a habit of saying '**s**' when I should have been saying '**z**'.

"*Non è s̲ucchero ma z̲ucchero*," they'd say but it all sounded the same to me.

I tried very hard to avoid the Italian word for rabbit. I found it virtually impossible to get my tongue round the '*gli*' in *coniglio*. While accepting their help with everyday vocabulary, I took umbrage when they picked me up on the supposedly mispronunciation of Michele's name.

"*Non è Michéle ma - Michele.*"

I was willing to learn but not at the expense of

wasting time over such trivialities as saying *e* instead of *é*. After the third or fourth time of being made to repeat 'Michele' – I stopped calling him by his Christian name in their presence and started calling him 'darling'.

*

I felt very proud when I finally held a conversation of more than three sentences with my teacher. There was a drawback, however; no one else spoke correct Italian – not even Michele. He informed me that the only people who did were teachers who taught Italian. Great, I thought. So, I stopped my Italian lessons and decided that probably, it would be more appropriate to take driving lessons instead. Michele, on the other hand, suggested I waited – just a bit longer – before enrolling at a driving school. But for how long? I was getting restless.

6

A Pet Pig and a Sneezing Hen

On my arrival at Michele's parents' house, they showed me a litter of newly born rabbits, hens and a pig that were kept in an outhouse. I had yet to discover that in the late 1970s animals were not kept as pets. Accustomed to having a menagerie in Poole, I assumed that here in Piussogno it was the same and so I gave the bunnies names and encouraged the hens to lay large eggs. The pig seemed quite friendly, too and I took on the job of feeding him scraps.

"Hello!" The pig trotted over to me and squealed in reply. I leaned over the fence and scratched its head.

"I think I'll call you Porky." 'This is bad news,' I thought to myself, 'I'm talking to a pig.' A dog would have been a better alternative, but I had no one else to converse with; Michele was working at the hotel in Como and Mara was doing her homework for the summer holidays.

The pig became my trusted confidant when I needed someone to talk to and tying a piece of rope around his neck, I often took him for walks up to the vineyards.

"Come on, Porky," I pulled gently on his makeshift lead and he grunted.

"Good job none of my English family or friends can see me now." I couldn't help giggling as he looked up at me before trundling ahead, occasionally snuffling in the grass. I innocently ignored the fact that Porky was not a family pet, but a source of food for the family.

Not long afterwards, I woke up to a hive of activity followed by a terrible scream from Porky. I decided it was time for me to go for a walk. No way could I watch my 'old friend' go under the knife. Politely refusing Michele's father's invitation to participate in the proceedings and learn how to make salami and sausages – I left them to it. If that wasn't bad enough, a few days later, I went outside to find the rabbits I'd watched grow-up, skinned and draped over the fence.

"*Coniglio arrosto, oggi*," Carla announced happily. Was she telling me *Rabbit Casserole* was on the menu today?

Michele's aunt was an exception to this rule, maybe because she didn't have children. She and *zio* had a cat that they allowed to come indoors and I invariably found the grey tabby curled up on the sofa fast asleep. Sometimes I'd find *zia* in the garden chatting away to herself.

"*Sto parlando con il gatto*," she explained, smiling and gesticulating to make me understand who she was talking to. Then I'd spot the cat lying under the tree.

One morning, I found her bustling around the hens.

"*Ciao, ho appena dato un' aspirina alla gallina marrone di là perché non sta bene. Credo che abbia preso un raffreddore.*"

Not sure whether she was teasing me or there'd been a complete breakdown in communication, I asked her to repeat what she'd said. Had she really given the brown hen an aspirin because she thought it had caught a cold? Then *zio* appeared shaking his head.

"*E' matta*," he said "*è completemente matta*."

Who's completely mad? Who was he referring to?

"*La gallina?*" I asked. I'd learnt the names of animals in Italian without any problem.

"*No, la zia!*" and off he went, shaking his head.

"*Sono sicura che stava starnutendo prima,*" said *zia*, giving me time to look up '*starnutire*' in my English/Italian dictionary.

"The hen was sneezing?" I asked in halting Italian. I was getting out of my depth now.

"*Sì, sì,*" *zia* answered but then her face creased into a smile as she saw my consternation. Delving into the deep pockets of her apron, she produced a small bottle of brandy and a packet of aspirin. More dialect and lots of gesticulating followed. I gathered she couldn't make up her mind which remedy would be best for her sick hen. I decided it was time to leave.

*

To have some quality time together at weekends, Michele and I went for walks up to the vineyards or around the village. Unlike Poole, there were no mansions or places of interest in Piussogno. The houses in the village were constructed on any private terrain, having received planning permission beforehand and grey stones were used as opposed to the familiar red bricks at home.

"How come stables and barns are next to houses? Doesn't anyone complain about the smell?" It didn't seem right to me.

"Nobody minds. They're all related and probably get free pieces of fresh meat and litres of fresh milk."

Most houses had the inevitable vegetable patch where vegetables and fruits of the season were grown to help the family economy and a small garden with flowers blooming in a haphazard fashion in splashes of bright colours.

"It's strange to see hens amongst flowers instead of plastic gnomes."

"Yes, but to us it's normal. *Weilà, ciao.*" A man slightly older than us came out of what looked like a stable and stopped in his tracks when he saw us.

"*Ciao!*" His face broke into a smile when he recognised Michele, who in turn introduced me to his friend. They spent the next five minutes catching up on each other's news and I did my best to ignore the putrid smell coming from the open door.

"*Vuoi vedere la mia stalla?*"

I suddenly realised Michele's friend had spoken to me.

"'E wants to know if you'd like to see 'is family's stable," Michele repeated for me.

"But shouldn't the cows be up the mountain?" I hadn't forgotten my cultural lesson on the train.

"They're going up next week."

I followed them inside and it became an experience that is imprinted on my memory forever – the odour and fresh manure everywhere were elements that had been missing from my education till then.

"Vuoi provare a mungere?" he asked me, gesturing with his hands.

"What? Would I like to milk a cow?" I turned to Michele for confirmation, afraid I'd misunderstood. Michele could hardly answer for laughing. I obviously declined the offer. My attire wasn't exactly that of a budding milkmaid and so, with Michele still laughing, we said goodbye and left.

Taking a different path this time, I heard the distinct sound of voices and water sloshing around as we neared the square.

"What's going on?" I walked faster and rounding the corner, I came face to face with a scene from a history book.

"I don't believe it – a real washing trough."

A group of women, sleeves rolled up, each clutching a bar of soap in one hand and a brush in the other, vigorously scrubbed clothes clean while passing on the local gossip. With flushed and animated faces from the physical exertion, water and soap suds splashed around them and voices became more excited when, I imagined, a particularly juicy piece of information was disclosed.

I noticed that the clothes being washed looked like working ones and the socks were the homemade knitted type.

"Do they put the rest of the laundry in the washing machine?" I asked Michele.

"Not everyone 'as a washing machine. A lot of people do their washing like this."

"Oh," I said, thankful that his parents had one.

Michele was right. On my way to the shop with Mara a few days later, we passed an old house with a cement washing trough alongside the railings in the front garden and the owner, a small, birdlike woman, armed with soap in one hand and scrubbing brush in the other, battled with her husband's underwear. I must have been too busy trying to talk to Mara to notice her before. She stopped when she saw us and acknowledged me with a slight nod and I smiled in reply. She wore her colourful headscarf tied under her chin and her flowery overall had damp patches over it from her energetic washing. She also had a very red nose.

"*Si chiama* Fabiola… *e le piace bere vino*," Mara told me confidentially, pretending to drink, as we walked past.

A few days later, we heard her mumbling away to herself and as we neared her gate, which had been left open, she shut it with a resounding clang.

"*Ecco!*" she said, pulling herself up to her full height and crossing her arms.

"*Adesso le mosche non possono entrare!*" Happy to think the flies couldn't get in with the gate closed, off she flounced, if a little unsteadily, back to her chore of washing her husband's string vests. It seemed she only rubbed the bar of soap over the holes – difficult to do at the best of times and I imagined it was a feat in itself for her to focus on the job in hand, especially after a midmorning tipple. Fabiola and her husband had a number of cats roaming around the garden and she praised them or scolded them according to her mood. On

73

my way to the bar one late afternoon, I saw her standing below the cherry tree, hands on hips, headscarf nodding vehemently. As I walked nearer, I heard her shouting to a kitten, mewing from one of the top branches.

"If you can't come down by yourself, don't think I'm coming to get you. I'm not – and you'll miss your dinner." When she saw me, she hurried over and told me that cats just didn't obey anymore. They had become quite a trial and she had better things to do than run after them. For one thing, there was her husband's washing to think about.

"*Mamma mia! Mamma mia!*" and off she went, rolling up her sleeves, ready for action.

Trying to keep a straight face, I walked on down to the square. I had something more important on my mind. Alberto needed cigarettes and as Mara had to help Carla in the vineyard, I offered to buy them. Confident that I would be able to make myself understood, I opened the door to the bar and stepped inside. Elderly men, in open-necked shirts, braces and dark corduroy trousers and a few I noticed wearing only string vests, white tufts of hair sprouting through the holes, sat at tables and chairs dotted around the room, playing cards while puffing on non-filter cigarettes. The two open windows tried ineffectively to filter out the thick, pungent smoke. Michele told me these men could make their *espressos* or *grappas* last all morning until the bells rang out at midday, reminding them it was time for lunch. Then the ritual would be repeated in the afternoon.

At the sight of a female walking in, they put their games on hold and followed my every move, grinning and nodding. Had my audience been a younger and more attractive one, I may have enjoyed the attention. As it was, I couldn't wait to escape.

"*Buonasera*," I muttered between clenched teeth, as I tried to find my way through a grey fog to the counter. I couldn't see Alda anywhere.

"*Oh, ciao*," she said in languid surprise appearing at last behind the glasses and bottles.

"*Ciao. Un pacchetto di Nazionali, per favore.*" I pronounced the words clearly, or so I thought.

"*Cosa?*" Her raised eyebrows and open mouth expressed her total lack of comprehension.

I repeated the phrase, even miming smoking a cigarette.

"*Ah, vuoi un pacchetto di Nazionali?*"

"*Sì, sì!*" I couldn't wait to have the offending packet of cigarettes in my hand.

'Good job I'm not in a hurry,' I thought to myself. Eventually she found the right box of cigarettes and extracted a packet for me.

"*Grazie. Ciao.*" I practically ran out into the fresh air.

"*Ciao*," she said as I shut the door.

Walking home, I reflected on village life and its simplicity: washing troughs, horse-drawn carts, the villagers. Could I adapt to this or would I soon miss reminders of town life? When I was with Michele I knew I wanted to be with him – but when I was alone…

7

Summer Days

Piussogno became a ghost town in July and August.

"Where is everyone?" I asked Michele one day.

"Oh, up the mountain." He waved vaguely towards the sky.

Most of the population owned a chalet in one of the mountains around us where temperatures were cooler and so they spent as much time as they could there.

"We 'aven't got a place up the mountain but you'll feel the difference in the air at Cercino," Michele told me, as we made our way up to the village above us in his father's Fiat. And, surprisingly enough, I did. Sitting outside, beneath the silver birches, sipping iced tea with Michele's cousin Nino and his Spanish wife Emily was sheer bliss. The fact that I couldn't hold a fluent conversation with them was irrelevant – just watching their two young children playing and the occasional nod and smile sufficed. I wanted to pack the slight breeze – non-existent in Piussogno – in the car and bring it back with us. I never wanted to go home after a few hours with Emily and Nino.

The week of 15th August is a holiday for everyone and

this particular day was a Bank holiday, called *Ferragosto*. Shops, factories and offices close and only a few food shops are open in the morning to sell fresh bread and cold meats. It's an excuse for families to get together and enjoy a day up the mountain. Michele came home for a week's holiday.

"Why am I so tired all the time?" I whinged to him.

"It's probably due to the change of air. Don't forget you've only been 'ere just over a month and you still 'ave to get used to temperatures of 40°."

I groaned. With the intense heat, came the flies. I'd never seen so many flies before. They settled on food and drink and then hid in bedrooms ready to disturb our night's sleep. One of the first items I bought that summer was a fly swat and I promptly forgot about my philosophy of not harming insects. Mosquitoes also proved to be a menace, lying in wait to bite you day and night. They seemed to find my English blood especially sweet.

The thought of spending a few hours in the shaded confines of ancient pines more than appealed to me and I couldn't wait to celebrate *Ferragosto*. At last, the day arrived and music and smells of fried sausages wafted down the mountain enticing people to come and dance and eat. Organisers set trestle tables with benches under the trees for the occasion and there was a *pista* for dancing. A band provided the music with a genuine accordion player and young and old alike danced together. Small children held hands and giggled, doing their best to imitate their elders, gyrating and sidestepping in time to the music. I felt quite excited.

"*Andiamo*," and before I knew it, Michele's father led me to the centre for a *mazurka*. I tried desperately to attract Michele's attention but just for a change, he was in deep conversation with a friend he hadn't seen for years. I had hoped to watch and maybe pick up a few ideas on how to dance *liscio* before joining in. But no, here I was swirling and twirling as if I'd done it all my life. It helped having a competent partner. Alberto guided me easily and I soon forgot my fears of making a spectacle of myself and enjoyed the music. A waltz followed and then a polka. All too soon, the last notes came to an end and we made our way back to Michele and the family.

Women sold bread rolls with fat sizzling sausages from a makeshift bar with portions of chips and wine flowed, inducing a great feeling of bonhomie. The men drank from a funny looking jug called *il mezzo*, and a wooden bowl known as *il ciapel*, passing it to each other and taking long dregs. Having lubricated their vocal chords, one of them started singing a local folksong and in unison the others joined in, women too, in an informal karaoke. Their melodious voices blended together as baritones, tenors, and contraltos sang passionately their favourite songs from the Valtellina.

"I've never heard anything so moving before," I whispered to Michele.

The singers had had no formal musical training but the sound was magical. No musical instruments accompanied them, either. The clear notes came from the heart. Not yet being able to understand the lyrics, I listened happily to the tunes, until Michele translated the words for me and I understood how melancholy they were:

Under the high mountains,
My mother rests in peace beneath the flowers.
The most beautiful and perfumed flowers,
From the mountains where I was born.

My mother is dead, I have to leave,
I have to leave and go to work.
And I have to leave my dear departed.
How can I take them those beautiful flowers?

"How can they sing these sad songs with such gusto?" It was a mystery to me. Perhaps the wine helped. Everybody knew each other and regarded these festivals as an opportunity to catch up on the latest news. I accepted the ritual of being hugged and kissed by complete strangers and then stared at. Being English meant being different from the villagers regardless of whether they accepted me or not. I just had to get used to it.

The festivals usually went on until the early hours of the morning, when the food had been eaten and the wine drunk. It's a wonder everyone managed to get home in one piece – but they did.

"How come children here manage to stay up so late?" I asked Michele.

"It's summer, they're on 'oliday. They go to bed when they're tired."

I glanced at my watch; 12.35am, then at the group of

children in front of us. They certainly showed no signs of fatigue.

"*Ciao!*" one little girl waved as she saw me looking at them.

"*Ciao!*" I smiled back. With a nod to her friends, she stood up and marched over to us.

"*Sei tu l'inglesina?*" she asked with her head cocked to one side.

Thanks to Luisa and my Italian lessons, I understood what she said.

"*Sì, sì.*" I told her.

"*Dai, dì qualcosa in inglese, ti prego.*"

"Right," I answered. "What's your name? Do you like…" She ran back to her friends laughing before I'd finished.

Michele shrugged and with a smile steered me towards a group of people who just happened to be more cousins.

*

Despite the torrid days, we still had pasta at midday and *minestra* in the evening. I craved for a ham salad and pickle sandwich. After a while, I found our daily diet tedious, to say the least. Never mind the different sauces to disguise it, and the fact that the pasta may come in different shapes and sizes, it's still *pasta*. I lost my apetite which did not go down well with Carla. In her eyes, I needed feeding up in order to beat the heat.

"*Dai, mangia ancora,*" was her mantra – and I obeyed,

picking up my fork once more and attacking yet another plate.

Almost without exception, after coffee, Mara whipped the cloth off the table and the men dealt the cards. We had to get into pairs for a game of *Briscola.* What a nightmare. I never seemed to be paired with Michele or Mara. The family took the game very seriously, but as I'd never really been interested in playing cards, I found it hard to feign enthusiasm. Everyone knew when I picked a winning card because I inadvertently let out a screech of delight. Unfortunately, it didn't happen very often.

With the hot summer days came the storms, invariably violent ones. Just after our arrival I experienced several terrifying thunderstorms. Both times we woke to a morning more humid than usual with an intangible presence around us.

"Ci sarà un bel temporale," announced Mara, looking at the threatening black sky. I gathered we wouldn't be able to go for our daily walk – and I was right.

Without any warning, I heard the first roll of thunder from behind the mountains and then lightning illuminated the skyline. Although spectacular to watch from closed windows, the thunder rumbling around the mountains and growing to a crescendo, it could also be quite frightening. I kept my fingers crossed I would never be alone at such a time. Raindrops fell one by one until the clouds appeared unable to hold them anymore – then the heavens opened. Now I understood why Italians had such incredibly big umbrellas. I put my little telescopic one away for holidays in England.

When hailstones the size of ice cubes fell, it spelled bad news for the farmers and their crops. A ritual of surveying the damage included the entire family. As soon as the storm had passed, we traipsed outside and gathered round the broken vines, shaking our heads and making suitable noises at the sight of the shrivelled up and battered grapes. I have always been able to mimic people and the Italian way of gesturing came naturally to me. I also love acting and all Italians are fine actors. Having said this, the aftermath was traumatic and a bit of drama was permissible.

One morning Alberto took my arm and pointed towards the mountain in front of us.

"*Guarda. Pioverà. Il Legnone ha il suo cappello.*" I turned to Pietro for a translation.

"*Legnone*'s the name of that mountain. When its peak is hidden by cloud, it's a sure sign that it's going to rain. We say '*Legnone has got its hat on*'."

"You're joking." Looking at the mountain in question in front of me, I found it hard to believe.

"No, honestly, you'll see. It'll rain before the day's over."

I couldn't help smiling. A few hours later, Pietro smiled at my incredulous expression when the sky darkened and the rain fell. I had to admit that the old wives' tale rang true.

Apart from Michele's young cousins who came to the house nearly every day, other regulars were three friends of Alberto. They had all fought in the Second World War and had ended up as prisoners in a concentration camp in Germany. Apparently, Alberto was lucky to have survived his ordeal. Only once did I ever hear him talk about that time. When his friends came to see him, they often reminisced about their feats when they, as partisans, fought the fascists. The wine appeared on the table with bread rolls, cheese and salami and the men lost themselves in their reveries. Their voices rose as each one recalled his own version of the facts.

"*Ricordate quando...* " Remember when... was one of the first phrases I learnt. This would herald the beginning of an episode that happened a life-time ago. The mountains around us had been home to various groups of partisans during the war years and ramshackle huts and stone ruins gave shelter to those hiding from the fascists. It wasn't always easy when families became divided by their political views. Their worst nightmare was to find themselves fighting against relatives and friends. A group from the village worked for the Resistance, helping prisoners cross the border into Switzerland. Danger played an integral role in their lives, survival being uppermost in their minds, as they hid in the mountains, overcoming freezing temperatures during the winter months and a desperate lack of food.

The partisans caught Mussolini with his mistress Claretta Petacci, at Dongo, a village by the lake not far from us, in April 1945. They had been trying to escape to Switzerland. Legend has it that Mussolini's treasure was thrown into Lake Como to prevent it falling into the wrong hands.

I used to be fascinated by these impromptu history lessons, often ignoring the horror of what they were saying. Only when their eyes filled with unwanted tears would the reality sink in. Then they would change the mood by remembering an anecdote, laughing and draining their glasses.

*

As promised, Remo turned up at the house one sultry evening to ask if we still wanted to go with him to see Daniela in St Moritz the following day. As it was a Saturday, we were free to join him. We arranged to leave early to give us time to look around and also to ring my mum and then meet Daniela for lunch.

Remo drove a big comfortable car and I settled in the back ready to enjoy the scenery. Unfortunately, I'd forgotten the fact that most Italians think they're Formula One drivers. As we lurched forward, all I saw was a blur.

"*Tutto bene?*" he asked after a while.

"Oh, yes, everything's fine," I answered, clutching my small gold cross on a chain around my neck.

As we went higher up the mountain, the air became fresher. Looking out of the window, I saw the river tumbling over large grey stones and in places the water was a deep green colour.

"*Prendiamo un caffè?*" Remo suggested as we reached the last bar before the Swiss border. We joined the other tourists drinking *espressos* and *cappucinos* before heading towards the Italian/Swiss Border or *Dogana*.

The Italian police waved us through, but the Swiss stopped each car and checked documents. They looked at my passport very carefully, studied the photo in detail and then my face before handing it back to me. They spoke a few phrases in Italian that I didn't understand and then waved us on our way.

"What did they say?" I asked Michele. "Do I look suspicious or something?"

"*Ma, no*," he answered, "they're probably just bored."

We filled up with petrol at the nearest station and I rang mum from the bar next to it. It was a surprise for her to hear my voice and a surprise for me to find her at home. Happy to know that all was well in the Baker family, we bought a supply of instant coffee and chocolate bars, and continued on our journey.

Quaint wooden chalets with trailing geraniums cascading from window boxes, stood out amongst tall firs and pines. Occasionally, we saw the odd herd of cows, each sporting large bells around their necks.

"Can we stop so I can take a photo?" I asked. "This is real Heidi country."

Remo seemed amazed by the fact that I wanted to photograph cows in a field on the way to St. Moritz, but he humoured me all the same. He parked by the verge and I snapped away – not only the animals grazing but also the snow-capped mountains, the chalets and the villages below us.

"Haven't you got mountains in your town?" he asked in Italian.

"No, only hills."

"Hmm," he needed time to digest this last piece of information. To him, a town without high mountains just didn't seem right somehow.

St. Moritz certainly lived up to its fame. The lake itself sparkled and the reflections on the still water mirrored the scenery to perfection. A few sailing dinghies glided over the surface and a motor boat passed in a flash, leaving a trail of frothy, white foam in its wake. We found the bar where Daniela worked and I took more photos of the town while we waited for her to finish. I recognised Daniela immediately. She was a female version of Remo; tall and slim with a ready smile.

"*Ciao!*" She held out her hand for me to shake then kissed me on both cheeks. She gave Michele and Remo more affectionate hugs and smackers but no way was I going to complain. I still had to get used to such displays of affection.

We lunched in a café by the lake with very attentive waiters and I couldn't help wondering how expensive our meal could be. I mean, St. Moritz is home to VIPs. I needn't have worried, after paying the bill both men left smiling. Daniela took us on a tour of her adopted town and I loved the shop windows, beautifully decorated to entice customers. I bought a souvenir to mark my very first trip there. We saw where the cable cars left to take skiers and tourists to the top of the town, and the Palace Hotel, home to the rich and famous during their holiday breaks. All too soon, however, Daniela had to begin her afternoon shift.

We found heavy traffic on the roads on our way home

and Remo had to drive at a leisurely pace. I didn't mind
– I enjoyed the view. As we drew nearer to Piussogno,
Michele looked at his watch and said:

"Good, we'll be 'ome in plenty of time for dinner."

"*Bene!*" replied Remo. Yes, food is a priority for
Italians.

8

A Little Blue Book

"Piussogno 'as a bar and four shops," Michele informed me.

His parents shopped at the grocer's owned by one of the wealthy families in the village and like most businesses here, they were family concerns.

"*Questa è Lina*," Mara introduced her to me as we walked through the door. Lina, a tall, thin woman in her late fifties, with long, grey hair pulled back in a bun, stopped serving and smiled at me, saying: "*Ciao. Ti piace qui?*"

I repeated the phrase Michele had taught me to let them know I couldn't speak Italian. She nodded before continuing to serve the woman in front of us. From the way they were chatting, it sounded more like a good natter than shop talk – and I was right. About ten minutes later, the customer remembered the reason for going to the shop. Pointing to two cheeses, she shrugged before rubbing her nose with an arthritic forefinger. Lina cut a sliver from both cheeses and handed them to the customer who nibbled first one then the other, before savouring the taste of the chosen one. I smiled to myself, doubting whether I'd ever witness such a scene in *my* home town. Lina bustled around picking up the items, clogs echoing on the tiled floor, as the villager reeled off her list.

While waiting our turn, I looked around the shop. From the outside, it appeared to be quite small but once inside, despite the lack of space and light, there seemed to be everything you could possibly need hidden away in cupboards and drawers that almost touched the ceiling. I presumed the ladder propped against the wall was ready to reach the higher levels. Different types of pasta came out of drawers, an assortment of cold meats was laid out in a fridge, together with cheeses of all shapes and sizes and fruit and vegetables had pride of place at the entrance. On future shopping trips, cakes and biscuits popped up from nowhere on request and even the more unusual items materialised. It was a mystery to me how they managed it. At last it was our turn and just as Lina asked Mara what she needed, an attractive girl with shoulder length black hair came through a door at the back of the shop.

"*Piera, questa è Valeria.*" Mara introduced us.

"Actually, I'm Valerie," I corrected, but it fell on deaf ears.

Piera, who looked a bit younger than me, helped her mother in the shop and her sister worked in the bar next door. She wanted to know where I came from in England and whether Poole was similar to Piussogno but she had to wait until I had mastered enough Italian to explain the infinite differences.

"Ma, perché hai lasciato un paese così bello?" she asked me several weeks later. She just couldn't understand why I'd left such a wonderful town for Piussogno.

"Michele." I answered but she shook her head, still not convinced.

"Ma, perché?" It just didn't seem possible that anyone in their right mind could leave behind a big and *meraviglioso* town like Poole for a mountain village so small that if you blinked when passing, you missed it. To be honest, there were days when I asked myself the same question.

Unlike the pay-as-you-buy system in England, here in the village shops, you don't hand over any money until the end of the month when the total is paid. The shop owner writes down everything in two small blue books: one for herself and one for the customer. Another characteristic of shopping is never to expect to be served quickly. Each customer has to have a chat to the shopkeeper and so the local gossip is passed on.

Mara went back to school in September and I had the job of going shopping each day. My days fell into a routine and the locals soon worked out what time I went to the shop.

"I don't understand why the shop's always full when I go in," I said, cuddling up to Michele before the rest of the family arrived. I was enjoying some rare quality time with him.

"Don't you?" he smiled. "I think it's because you're English and don't forget, not a lot 'appens 'ere usually." He kissed the top of my head and I wished we could have more moments like this.

"You know your mum gives me a list when I go shopping? Well, I wanted to try asking for the articles myself but as soon as I open my mouth, everyone stops talking until I finish. The other day, they all nodded and smiled. I think I must be making progress."

"Certainly, you are," Michele laughed.

"And another thing," I pulled him closer, kissing him back. "I don't like the way the women look at my stomach all the time. Do they all think I'm pregnant or something? Chance would be a fine thing." I couldn't help adding, thinking about his parents relaying last minute messages to Michele when we'd already gone to bed.

Admittedly, I did put on a considerable amount of weight after my arrival but since I'd learnt to say I only wanted one plate of pasta, I hadn't gained any extra pounds. There had been no mention of an impending wedding either, and for the more devout villagers, this was cause for concern.

"Well, let them think it. We know you're not. They're probably wondering why we 'aven't set a date for our wedding, though. We'll 'ave to talk about that."

A fit of coughing, followed by a blast of loud dialect warned us that Alberto and Carla had finished working on the vines and when they walked in, they found us sitting demurely on the sofa engrossed in the television.

*

I hadn't considered my dietary needs to be that important until I came to Piussogno.

"I really miss my cornflakes," I confessed to Michele one morning. "All I want is a bowl of cornflakes with a large cup of Nescafé and a slice of toast with marmalade."

"Um, I don't think the shops 'ere cater for the English tourist," Michele seemed genuinely sorry for me.

This time, Lina couldn't help me. No packets of cornflakes lurked in the depths of her store. After much searching, we finally found packets of Kellogg's cornflakes in a shop in Sondrio, the county town, about 25kms away. Michele's friend, Adriano bought a supply for me each time he went to Sondrio on business. Apparently, the assistant had asked him if he was buying it for a hotel but he'd replied blandly that it was just for an English friend.

*

Not that you would have known it but another shop stood almost next door to Lena's. To me it looked like any other house at first sight. Only the front door with heavy shutters at the top made it different from the rest. A bell rang as I opened the door and a strong smell of camphor invaded my nostrils. Like the grocer's, the interior was small and dark with fabrics, cottons, buttons and wool of every colour overflowing from boxes of varying dimensions stacked on shelves. Overalls, skirts, trousers, shorts and underwear peeped out of larger boxes stored on more shelves on the opposite side. A ladder leaned against the wall ready to reach the boxes that were practically touching the ceiling.

The sound of wooden clogs clumping on the tiles startled me. I turned to see an elderly lady, so elderly that I wondered if she'd be able to serve me. Her grey hair was pulled into a tight bun and she wore a dark blue dress. She had piercing blue eyes that gave the impression of reading your mind and I tried desperately to clear mine of any impure thoughts.

"*Ah, buongiorno,*" she croaked, staring pointedly at my stomach.

"*Buongiorno,*" I replied, returning her stare. "*Ho bisogno di un filo blu, per favore.*" I hoped she understood my stumbling Italian for some blue cotton and she did. I willed the cotton to be at ground level because I didn't want to be responsible for sending her up the ladder at her age.

"*Un momento solo,*" she answered, moving the ladder to the opposite side of the shop then she hoisted up her dress and climbed the rungs to the top before I had time to say "Be Careful!" Balancing a large box on the ladder, she took out a dark blue cotton reel to show me.

"*Sì, sì,*" I nodded and my mouth dropped open as I watched her slide down the ladder. Where did she get her agility from?

"*Hai bisogno di qualcos'altro?*" a shrewd businesswoman, she wanted me to buy more than a mere cotton reel.

"*No, grazie,*" I had no intention of buying anything else, "*E' tutto.*"

An assortment of toys and sweets sat haphazardly on the counter next to the till. Instead of ringing up the price of the cotton on the cash register, she deftly picked up the pen and notepad by the side and made a quick note. Noticing my puzzled expression, pointing to the till, she explained she didn't trust these new-fangled contraptions, preferring to do the sums in her head. After saying goodbye, she clattered back to the dim void of the back room and I made my way out, stepping over balls, buckets and spades and toy cars that I hadn't noticed before. A tactic I realised later, to encourage young mums to buy a little something for their offspring. The toddlers couldn't resist the temptation of picking up a toy on the way out of the shop and to avoid a tantrum, mums would follow Gemma's suggestion of making the children happy.

'That's an incredible example of child psychology from a woman who I doubt had had more than Primary education.' I thought.

Unlike Lina's grocer's that had customers whatever time you went, Gemma's shop was usually empty. Not one to gossip, her main aim in life was to sell as much as she could – small talk didn't form part of her agenda.

"Does Gemma decide the price of her goods?" I asked Michele as we strolled arm-in-arm down to the bar to buy an ice-lolly.

"Why? Did she overcharge you for something?"

"Well, I'm not really one to judge, am I? Until I learn enough basic Italian and understand dialect, I haven't a clue what people say to me half the time. No, it's just that when I went to buy some wool for your mum, I saw a manicure set and I asked her how much it was. I mean, nothing's priced at all. She thought about it for a minute then said it cost eight thousand lire. I got the impression she decided how much to charge items as she sold them. It sounded quite expensive, so I didn't buy it."

Then I remembered something else.

"When I walked in, Gemma actually had a customer and they lowered their voices – which they needn't have done – but anyway, she suddenly disappeared through the door to the back of the shop and emerged with packets of pasta and biscuits. Has she got her own black market business for discreet customers?"

"Maybe she doesn't want to upset Lina by selling groceries, too," Michele reasoned. I wasn't convinced.

Gemma hoped I would join the ranks of her loyal clientele who always left the shop with more than they actually wanted but I refused to fall victim.

Just after I officially become *Signora Barona,* I went to buy a zip for my tightest jeans which fitted me once more.

"*Che ne dici di comprare un bel peluche pronto per il bebé?*" Gemma resorted to speaking to me in Italian as opposed to the accepted dialect in an attempt to entice me to buy something else.

"*No, grazie.*" I replied firmly. I had no intention of becoming pregnant and putting on weight just yet. My mum always maintained that I am a very obstinate person and I can now say she's right. Gemma lost her touch with the *inglesina.*

One Saturday evening, Adriano and Luisa invited Michele and me for a meal and not wanting to go empty handed, I took the opportunity of suggesting that we bought a cake from the rival grocer's on the main road as I'd yet to see what it was like. I loved it as soon as we walked in. The glass front made it lighter and gave the impression of being bigger than Lina's. Articles sat neatly on shelves all within easy reach and the groceries seemed fresher to me.

'This is more like home,' I thought to myself.

"*Buongiorno*," Giovanna, a woman in her fifties, smiled warmly. Unlike her contemporaries, she sported a short hairstyle and wore fashionable clothes under a smart overall to keep them clean and she had comfy but stylish shoes.

"Giovanna's 'usband is a builder and works away all week, 'e comes 'ome at weekends," Michele explained. "They've got two married sons who live in the flats above them."

Looking around the shop, I saw a highchair in the corner with a chubby toddler strapped in it munching on a roll.

"*Ciao*," I said to him, receiving a happy gurgle in reply.

"*E' il mio nipote*," Giovanna hurried over to explain and Michele translated for me.

"'E's 'er grandson and when she 'as to babysit, Davide stays in the shop with 'er."

I often found Davide with Giovanna when I had the chance to go there. He lapped up the attention from customers and accepted pieces of bread, sweets and lollipops with a smile. Giovanna always made me feel welcome and treated me like a regular customer even though I didn't have a blue book with her. As well as being efficient, she still had time to chat to her customers, listening to their problems and offering advice when asked. I definitely preferred buying from her.

*

Growing up in a fairly large town of around 250,000 inhabitants, offering every facility possible for young and old, I had to come to terms with not being able to do much in such a small village. I couldn't even go window-shopping. In fact, I couldn't go very far at all. A quick walk around Piussogno only took half an hour. I was getting restless and I also needed some new clothes. I inevitably put on weight due to my Mediterranean diet and despite the illusion of breathing in and convincing myself that I could do the zip up if I didn't exhale or sit down, in the end I still needed a new pair of trousers. Michele suggested we went to Morbegno with Pietro the following morning.

"Can't we go shopping after lunch instead?" I asked.

"We'll 'ave to wait till four when the shops open."

"What?" I couldn't believe they closed for lunch and a sleep.

"They stay open till 7.00 in the evening, you know."

"Who wants to go shopping then?" I had assumed that shops in the towns opened from 9am to 5pm and only the village shops had their own opening times. Anyone could go shopping during their lunch hour if shops were open all day. I was too English to appreciate the Italian culture of lunch and a siesta being more important than something as essential as shopping. Still, I didn't want to miss the chance of going to town, so we arranged to go after breakfast.

"Look, there's *il Ponte Vecchio* over there," Michele said as we drove over the River Adda. I remembered seeing the old bridge when we arrived. We parked near the station and arranged to meet Pietro later.

I fell in love with the town as soon as I saw it. The women we passed wore fashionable clothes and sported the latest hairstyles and the men were equally well-groomed. The shops, all within walking distance, lined along three main streets, boasted decorative window displays cleverly and tastefully set out to entice customers. As we sauntered along, Michele told me that most of the shops were family concerns, which was fine unless of course they'd just had a 'domestic'. I picked up on the signs when we entered a newsagent's. The couple vied for our attention and treated us like royalty, which seemed a bit ridiculous considering we only wanted to buy a newspaper.

"If we'd bought something more expensive, we could 'ave got a discount," Michele said as we left. "I think they were in the middle of a serious row." In Italy, there's no such thing as hiding your feelings, not even in front of complete strangers. Italians are far too passionate for that.

Michele took me to a renowned boutique that was perhaps considered to be one of the best in Morbegno at the time, not to mention the most expensive.

"Buongiorno! Che cosa desidera?" I always translated it as *What do you desire?* Instead of *What do you want?* The assistant, immaculately dressed with equally immaculate make-up, swooped down on us and when Michele explained what we wanted, pairs of different coloured trousers appeared as if by magic delicately draped over one slender, tanned arm, along with various blouses.

"Can't I just browse by myself?" I asked Michele.

"No," he answered. "The assistants are 'ere to 'elp the customer."

After years of walking into English chain stores with friends and choosing outfits together, it came as a shock to find myself hounded by an assistant who chose clothes for you, guided you to the changing rooms, pulled back the curtains with no warning to assure it was a perfect fit and encouraged you to buy, regardless of whether it really suited you or not.

'Right,' I decided, 'style is fundamental to Italians and naturally you have to pay for it. If this means service on a one-to-one basis, then I intend making the most of it.' I tried on different combinations, shocked at how much extra flesh I'd acquired since my arrival in Piussogno, but enjoying the chance to experience the subtle feel of soft silk and cool cotton against my skin, totally ignoring the number of noughts after the figure on the price tag. I had no intention of wasting money on clothes – or so I thought. Without really knowing how, I found myself clutching an ostentatious carrier bag holding an overpriced pair of brown trousers and an equally costly sky-blue blouse. Italian assistants had a way of flattering the customer and it had certainly worked with me. Michele told me not to worry because being good quality, they would last a long time – which really meant he wouldn't have to come shopping with me for a while. With this in mind, he glanced at my sandals and suggested that perhaps it would be wise for me to buy a comfortable pair of walking shoes and I agreed.

"I'll take you to the shop I always used to go to."

"Will it still be there?" I mean, after seven years it could have shut down or changed hands.

"This is Morbegno, remember. Of course it'll still be there."

I said no more.

As we reached the shop, we saw a handwritten sign on the door: *Torno subito!*

"What does that mean?"

"It means *Back soon!*" Michele replied, lighting a cigarette, completely unfazed. "Per'aps 'e's gone for a coffee or is just late opening this morning."

Another lesson for me to learn: never be surprised if the shop owners open later than the time stated on the door or they close the shop if they have a more pressing engagement. We waited and waited and after fifteen minutes, I felt sorely tempted to leave a note with an explanation of *Back soon!*

"How about buying my shoes another day?" I suggested. Stubbing out his cigarette, Michele nodded. "We'll go to the Market." Saturday was Market day in Morbegno and St. Anthony's Square, used as a car park during the week, became a hive of activity as stalls were erected early in the morning. Moving up and down the aisles, I couldn't understand why the stallholders seemed to shout at possible customers instead of enticing them in soft tones to buy. Well-built women with huge overflowing shopping bags pushed and shoved.

"Ouch!" I couldn't help the outburst as a young woman with a pushchair literally rammed into my ankles as she attempted to get by.

"*Pardòn*," she said apologetically.

"Did she say 'pardon'?" The pain was forgotten as I clung to the hope of maybe finding another English speaker.

"No, it's another way of saying 'sorry'. Look at these *polenta* pans…" Michele was more interested in a set of copper pots in varying sizes. The stalls sold everything: food, clothes, bed linen, tablecloths, tea towels, cutlery, crockery, toys, tools, even animals and birds. You name it they sold it.

Suddenly, two stallholders began yelling at each other.

"Quick. Let's get out of here. There's going to be a fight." I tried to pull Michele away.

"What are you talking about?" he said, laughing. "They're not arguing. That man over there simply asked 'is friend if 'e wanted to go and see the football match at the bar with 'im tonight. They're deciding which bar to go to."

"Well, you could have fooled me." I would never have classed it as everyday conversation. What was it like when they had a serious argument, then?

As Michele led the way through the stalls, I marvelled at the way the wares had been displayed to the best possible advantage in such a small amount of space. Compared to shop prices, it was cheaper to buy from the Market even though the quality of the goods was no different. Apparently, you could exchange articles of clothing if they weren't the right size the following week. Having seen all the Market had to offer we headed up a narrow road with more shops on either side.

"Now you're going to see something different. This is one of the oldest shops in Morbegno," Michele told me as we went into what looked like any other grocer's.

We exchanged pleasantries with the owner, who then offered to give us a tour of the place. Leaving his son in charge, we walked through what I assumed to be a storeroom at the back of the shop.

"Wow!" I never expected to find myself in a real Aladdin's Cave. Shelves full of wooden toys and utensils completely covered the walls. Brightly painted cars, trains and aeroplanes, intricately made and perfect in every detail, waited proudly for a buyer.

"*Sono fatti a mano*," the man explained but this time, I didn't need Michele to translate. You could see the toys were all handmade. Colourful wooden garden paraphernalia covered the floor: wheelbarrows, buckets, pots, vases of all shapes and sizes. The owner explained that tourists loved discovering this secret room and usually ended up going home laden.

"Do you think we ought to buy something?" I hissed in Michele's ear but before he could answer, the man marched on ahead inviting us to follow. In the dimly lit room, I could just make out a flight of stairs at the far end.

"Where's he taking us?" I asked just as a very strong smell of cheese wafted up from hidden depths below. We found ourselves inside a cellar. The air felt cooler here. Different types of cheeses filled the shelves and on the opposite side there were rows and rows of bottles of wine. He gave us a short description of them and where they came from before taking us down a shorter flight of steps that led to the wine cellar. Huge wine vats stood next to each other and the air held the piquant smell of vintage wine. Just by inhaling, I felt positively intoxicated. He and Michele became engrossed in the serious business of winemaking and then the owner offered him a glass of wine which he accepted happily. No way could we leave empty-handed, so I bought several wine jugs for my family and a couple of wooden decorations for the garden that I knew my mum would like. Thanking the owner profusely for allowing us to share the wonders of his shop, we came out and headed to the bar for a coffee with Pietro.

"I really like Morbegno," I said linking arms with Michele. "It makes me feel more at home."

Michele gave me a quizzical look. I hated myself for admitting it but I preferred the way the people dressed and the fact that the women wore make-up and expensive perfume. I saw Morbegno as a way of recharging my batteries, so to speak, but to get there I needed transport.

"Darling," I said as we sipped our *espressos* at a table

underneath a huge umbrella, outside one of the bars while waiting for Pietro, "I think it's time I learned to drive."

"Okay," he realised the time had come for me to get behind the wheel and deep down, he knew the reason why.

9

Mobile at Last

I discovered almost immediately that I couldn't rely on the public transport system in Piussogno. A bus went to Morbegno in the morning and again in the afternoon. I had never thumbed a lift in my life and had no intention of doing so now. Having mastered the Italian language enough to venture out alone, thanks to Luisa, the obvious alternative was to learn to drive and I felt ready to take to the roads – out of necessity more than anything else. So, I enrolled at a driving school in Morbegno that just happened to be a family concern. Signor Pizzini, a small, wiry man in his fifties with a shock of grey hair and a grey moustache that twitched into his nostrils when he spoke, doubled as teacher and driving instructor. His wife was the secretary and his son and cousin were driving instructors, too.

"You have to attend theory lessons for a month and pass the written test before you can actually start having driving lessons." He barked at me in clipped Italian, before turning to Michele to tell him how much it would cost.

"Okay," I said, trying not to shake.

About twenty of us aged between eighteen and thirty arrived for our first lesson and found *Signor* Pizzini waiting for us. We took our places and took out the regulation Highway Code theory quiz book that had been given to us after paying the enrolment fee. I sat next to a young girl who introduced herself as Sonia.

"I'm English and my knowledge of the Italian language is very basic," I explained to her in faulting Italian.

"Don't worry," she had a friendly smile and deliberately spoke slowly which put me at ease. "We can study together if you like." Our conversation stopped abruptly, however, when our instructor took to the floor.

The theory lesson began and I started to panic. How would I ever learn enough to pass the exam? He spoke so quickly that I wondered how he could breathe at the same time. Naturally, I only managed to understand two or three words in every phrase. It took me less than five minutes to see that it would be inconceivable to even consider taking notes. His mannerisms and gesticulating fascinated me. It seemed a physical impossibility for him to stay still. He raised his voice, giving the impression that he could only deliver words by shouting. When he asked a question, he expected an answer and if it was wrong, more ranting and raving followed. Fortunately, he never made me the target of his questions.

He used a projector to explain the ins and outs of the Highway Code and as I became more familiar with the terminology, I found out that, in fact, he was a very good teacher. A break in each lesson allowed smokers to relax with a cigarette while Sonia and I took the opportunity of going over various aspects of rules just learnt and she explained anything I hadn't understood. It came as no surprise, of course, that I had to study twice as hard as everyone else. Every evening I revised the Highway Code and then tried doing the quizzes. The answers were at the back of the book, so I could check my progress. Michele accused me of cheating when he saw that I hardly made any mistakes which didn't impress me. My father had always taught us the saying: "If a job's worth doing – it's worth doing well." I shot him a look that needed no words and returned to my studying. Michele took the hint and went back to his sports paper.

Sonia and I met up once a week to study, Pietro chauffeuring me to and fro as Michele was working. She was married with a toddler and with her husband working away during the week she desperately wanted to learn to drive. We spent a couple of hours doing the quizzes and then stopped for *merenda* – as the Italians call an afternoon snack.

As the day of the theory exam loomed nearer, the tension grew and voices were raised during the lessons. I surprised everyone at our last meeting by voluntarily answering a question – correctly. There followed a brief pause before the instructor bellowed out:

"*Brava, brava!*" Despite all eyes focusing on me in total amazement, I felt ready for the exam.

We arrived early on the day, talking and joking about anything but the impending examination paper. I expected the exam to be taken in a spacious room, sitting on our own, to avoid any kind of cheating. Instead, we continued to sit in our usual places, in the same classroom, next to our friends. The examiner from Sondrio, the county town, arrived and took his place at the desk. Having distributed the exam papers, the instructor told us to begin and then he walked up and down, looking at our answers, shaking his head or nodding, depending on whether we had correctly put a tick or a cross in the box, while the examiner continued to read his sports paper. I must admit that I spent quite a while watching him. If only I had had such a teacher for my 'O' levels and 'A' levels. An hour later, we stopped writing and handed in our papers.

"Come back in an hour when the tests will have been marked," *Signor* Pizzini told us.

Naturally, we all headed for the nearest bar for a much-needed *cappuccino* and as if by mutual agreement, nobody mentioned the theory exam. At the given time, we traipsed back to the driving school. The examiner was still sitting at the desk at the front of the room, but the *Gazzetta dello Sport* was now neatly folded under a pile of papers. One by one, he distributed the papers and I noticed that mine had *orale* written at the top of the page. My instructor explained that being a foreigner, I had the chance of an oral exam had I made more than four mistakes. As it was, I hadn't made any at all. The head-shaking and nodding was forgotten and surprisingly enough, we had all passed! Now, at long last I could start driving lessons and not wanting to waste time, I arranged for a lesson the following afternoon.

My driving instructor, turned out to be none other than *Signor* Pizzini. I didn't know whether to laugh or cry. But, despite his fiery manner, he excelled at his job – or so I was told. He also expected to have the road to himself when he took learners out for the first time. I will never forget my first driving lesson with him. I climbed into the Fiat 127 quite happily, excited to get behind the wheel at last. Having adjusted the rear mirror and seat position, I put my seat belt on and practised using the pedals and gear stick. Following the instructions given, I then turned the ignition, pushed the gear stick into first and slowly edged forward. At least, that was the general idea. Instead, the car jerked ahead, eliciting a torrent of incomprehensible Italian from my instructor. I had been warned that *Signor* Pizzini could make the hardest of people cry, such was his wrath. I had an advantage; in my case it was ignorance of the language. Despite his menacing dialect and arm-waving, I continued to crawl along the main road.

When we came to the traffic lights, he told me to stop the car. He then told me to get out to see how far I was from the pavement. The fact that it was a Saturday afternoon, the traffic lights were green and a queue of cars was forming behind us was irrelevant. I cringed. My patience was dwindling. After much twitching and gesturing, I was allowed back into the car and we continued the lesson. I wanted to ask the reason for the outburst but then thought better of it.

I had another instructor – his cousin – for my second lesson. His manner was anything but reassuring and I became so nervous that at one point I accelerated instead of braking, and as we were at a junction there could have been repercussions. We were lucky. Only one car was coming in the opposite direction and unlike most Italians, was driving slowly. I said a silent prayer and made a mental note of the expressions used by the driving instructor.

"*Santo cielo*" was perhaps the only phrase fit to repeat.

It didn't come as a surprise when I found myself once more with *Signor* Pizzini. This time I was ready for anything. He growled the route I had to take and almost immediately began to complain about my driving skills. I listened to his verbal flow for a while and then I stopped the car.

Looking him squarely in the eyes – and hoping he couldn't see me shaking – I told him in my best Italian: "If I knew how to drive, I wouldn't be sitting next to you now having a lesson, would I?"

I waited for yet another outburst, but instead he returned my stare and started to laugh.

"*Brava, tusa.*"

After that, we got on really well and he affectionately referred to me as *tusa*, which is dialect for 'girl'.

However, driving lessons in Italy differed drastically to those given in England. I didn't realise it at the time, but all I learned was how to change gears, drive without hitting the car in front, and stop the car at junctions and traffic lights without stalling the engine. I didn't practise hill starts, u-turns, emergency stops or how to reverse into a parking space which I still haven't mastered after more than 30 years behind the wheel. When talking to a friend later, she told me that the rest came with practise.

When the date of the exam appeared on the board, seven of us decided to go for it. I felt quite confident before climbing into the driver's seat and meeting the glare of the examiner. Not even an encouraging wink from *Signor* Pizzini, who, in accordance with Italian law, joined us in the back seat for the exam, could make me feel better.

It came as no surprise when he told us we had failed.

"In your case, it's the car driving you. Try again when you can drive the car," he snarled at me.

"You should have adjusted your glasses before driving off," he told another.

"Why didn't you guess the car in front was going to stop suddenly?" he shouted at another... and so it continued. By no means impressed, either, *Signor* Pizzini immediately booked us for the next available exam the following month. We all decided to go to our local bar to drown our sorrows with a *cappuccino* and a cake.

We turned up earlier than usual for our driving test and those who wanted a last minute lesson were given one. Signor Pizzini gave me his favourite piece of advice:

"Whatever you do – don't stall the engine!"

I nodded and crossed my fingers.

This time a different examiner came and, seeing his ready smile and reassuring manner, we all breathed a sigh of relief.

As I waited for my turn, however, the sky darkened and the heavens opened. I don't like thunderstorms at the best of times and this seemed an omen. I drove off with lightning flashing and thunder rolling menacingly around the mountains. At the traffic lights it happened – I stalled the engine. Without thinking I said in English:

"Oh, no! I don't believe it!"

"*Calma, tusa. Accendi di nuovo. Va tutto bene,*" Signor Pizzini tried to put me at ease.

I was not convinced. How could everything be fine? Anyway, I did as I was told, I turned the key, the engine spluttered back to life and I finished the route, stopping outside the hospital, of all places, as directed. The examiner wished me all the best.

"*Grazie,*" I replied, slightly confused.

"I mean, enjoy driving," he explained.

"I've passed?" I couldn't believe it.

"*Sì, tusa. Sì, sì!*" Signor Pizzini patted me on the shoulder.

I'd passed. In fact, we all passed and *Signor* Pizzini was more than satisfied. This time we were able to celebrate over a *cappuccino* and a *brioche*.

Now Michele and I could think about buying a second-hand car. We had been using his dad's Fiat 500 but now we needed our very own car. No way did I want a brand new one to begin with. Not that I didn't feel confident on the roads – it was just that every driver seemed to have his own highway code.

I still couldn't accept the fact that it was not compulsory to wear seat belts. What had been a ritual during driving lessons was quickly forgotten once the driving test had been passed. People thought I was very odd the way I religiously fastened my seat belt every time I got in the car or any car, come to that.

"Have you no faith in your driving skills or those of other drivers?" They asked me quite seriously. No one seemed to take into consideration the fact that it was a precaution against serious injury in the case of an accident.

I soon discovered that there was a revised version of the Italian Highway Code:

- *Never overtake unless there is an element of risk: a blind corner, or a car speeding in the opposite direction.*
- *Cyclists are considered obstacles to overtake at the very last minute.*
- *The cardinal sin is to respect the speed limit.*
- *Remember to stop in the middle of the road for a chat if you spot a friend you haven't seen for a long time. Don't worry about the queue forming behind you, furiously hooting – ignore them.*
- *Never stop at a pedestrian crossing to let anyone cross the road. (The first time I did exactly that, I was hooted at from behind and the two women waiting on the kerb, looked at me blankly as if I were mad and would accelerate as soon as they stepped into the road.)*
- *Don't slow down when approaching a set of traffic lights that is turning to amber – instead accelerate. I did just that once and stopped, only to hear a mouthful of abuse from the driver behind who was in a hurry. Had it been winter with the windows firmly shut and the hot air furiously blowing, I'd have been none the wiser, but it was a very*

sultry summer's afternoon, the windows were down and tempers were frayed.

- *Courtesy on the road means waving to someone you know. It doesn't mean giving way to another driver or allowing a car to pass.*

Road rage, I suspect, originated on the continent. Italians, in particular, have always been known for their fiery temper and menacing gestures. I'm afraid that I have since joined the ranks and gesticulate like the rest of them. The old saying – *if you can't beat them, join them* – rings true. Of course, nowadays, Italian drivers wear seatbelts and respect the laws regarding the authentic Highway Code. With the recent introduction of a points system, nobody wants to lose his or her driving licence and have to rely on public transport – no way.

10

A Protestant Amongst the Catholics

Religion proved to be another problem I had to face when I first arrived in Italy. I had been brought up in the Anglican Church and was a Protestant, but, as Michele was a regular churchgoer and the priest had no objections, I went with him. Walking into *Santa Margherita*, I noticed that the men were sitting on the left-hand side of the church, and the women on the right. Having been used to staying together as a family in England, I had no intention of doing otherwise in Italy.

"Don't think I'm going to sit by myself," I hissed into Michele's ear.

We raised a few eyebrows as I sat beside Michele and several remarks were made but I looked firmly in front of me and waited for the service to commence. In the weeks that followed, I noticed that other young females took to sitting in the pews on the left.

The priest, Don Giulio, a jovial man in his late thirties, exuded what a man of the cloth should be, a people's priest, there for everyone. Young and old alike seemed to vie for his attention. Short and stout, with olive skin and a shock of tight black curls, his dark, brown eyes peered through a pair of thick black glasses. He walked with a purpose and rarely wore his dog collar. A small, gold crucifix on his lapel gave the only clue that he was a priest. He enjoyed socialising and a glass of wine never went amiss. It was thanks to him that Michele and I were able to marry at St George's, my parish church in Poole.

We had originally agreed that I'd stay in Piussogno for a while before deciding whether I could make it my home or not but our plans had to be changed as I could only legally stay as a tourist for three months.

"We'd better go to the British Consul in Milan to see what they suggest." Michele said. So, he asked his boss for a day off work, and on the last Friday in August, he took me on the train to Milan. I needed a day in Milan to break the monotony of village life. As we walked hand-in-hand to the British Consul offices, I revelled in the heady chaos that only cities breed, enjoying the noise of traffic and mixing with fashionable pedestrians.

Having explained my predicament, a very competent British official asked me if I had an Italian boyfriend.

"Yes, we're engaged." I answered.

"Well, then. Marry him and you've solved your problems."

"Is it really that easy?" Michele and I looked at each other, raising our eyebrows in unison.

The fact that we were different denominations meant that no way could we marry in a Catholic church here in Italy, and I had set my heart on a religious ceremony with all the trimmings. Don Giulio came to the rescue. He told us he'd ask for approval from the Vatican for us to marry in my parish church in Poole. A concession that more than appealed to my family and me, the only setback being that I had to delegate my mum to arrange my wedding. Each time I needed to speak to her on the phone, Michele and I had to drive over the border to Switzerland. These soon became weekly trips.

"The Vicar said he can marry you on 12th November. Is that all right with you?" Mum said, in organisation mode.

"That's fine." Although I'd dreamed of having a spring wedding, we were no longer in a position to choose.

Don Giulio asked me if I wanted to become a Catholic, but on principle, I declined his suggestion to convert to Catholicism and after emphatically repeating my views as to why I intended remaining a Protestant, he accepted my decision without further discussion and set about writing to Rome immediately.

The announcement of our impending wedding in November put paid to the pagan virtue of living in sin, especially amongst the older villagers, who decided that maybe I wasn't so different after all.

*

The church of *Santa Margherita* had no organ but a group of children sitting at the front, started the hymns. They sang remarkably well and in tune considering they never practised beforehand. The female Sunday worshippers filed into church with plenty of time to spare before the service began and the more devout among them took out rosaries and expertly passed the beads through their fingers. The men, however, stayed outside huddled together in small groups until one of the altar servers rang the bell outside the vestry. They traipsed in as the opening hymn rang round the church and squeezed into the pews like sardines.

Don Giulio never seemed to mind the endless chatter among the congregation. He simply raised his voice a fraction and glanced up to the heavens, as if invoking celestial help before resuming the Mass. As if they didn't spend enough time chattering at the bar, the elderly men continued their conversations in church: the weather and its effects on the produce growing at the time; whether this year's grape harvest would be better than the last one, and whose wine would taste the best; the economic situation; their pensions; and so it went on. The women discussed more important things before the service started such as:

"What are you having for Sunday lunch?" and

"Oh no. Did I turn off the gas or not?" or

"Who's that person in the front pew?" and

"Look at so-and-so's new outfit, bet it cost a lot and she was supposed to be saving up to buy a second-hand car."

When it was time to file up the aisle to the altar to take communion, the older women literally elbowed their way to the front and stuck out their tongues for the *ostia*. (wafer). As is the practice in the Roman Catholic Church, no wine was ever given; only the priest had that privilege.

Being the only Protestant in a dominant Catholic community was naturally a topic of conversation.

- Was I a Christian?
- Did I believe in God?
- Why didn't I go to confession?
- But why couldn't I take communion? No, it was impossible that Protestants were religious.
- And what would happen if I were to have children, what denomination would they be?
- Did I believe in *Maria* or *La Madonna*, as she was called in Italy?

After each Sunday service I would be inundated with questions. Michele helped out until I could express myself intelligibly. A lot of the younger church members liked the Protestant doctrine:

"What, you have wine with the wafer at communion?"

"There's no confession?"

"Don't tell me there's no rosary to recite!"

"This is a *cool* religion."

At this point, afraid that some parents might see me as a threat to their children who were preparing for their First Communion ceremony, I quickly made it known that should I have children, they would be brought up as practising Catholics. An almost audible sigh of relief was heard throughout the adult community.

Another peculiarity of the church is the fact that every day is dedicated to one or more saints. "*Auguri.*" I heard this word almost on a daily basis and soon guessed the meaning of it. Most of the villagers were named after a saint and friends and neighbours wished them a *Happy Day*.

Even though the church in Piussogno is called *Santa Margherita*, it is dedicated to *Sant' Antonio*. However, I decided not to ask too many questions for the time being about why the church wasn't called *Sant' Antonio*. Michele pointed out his statue to me, kept in a prominent glass case, near the altar.

"It's always taken out the week before the festival and put on a table, ready for the procession in the afternoon," Michele explained. "The *Festa di Sant'Antonio* is on the second Sunday in June and everyone looks forward to 'aving a good time. After the morning service, cakes and wine are auctioned. One of the men takes charge and standing on a chair, 'e shouts out a price and 'opes someone will start bidding."

It sounded fascinating and I was sorry I'd missed it.

"Don't worry," Michele said "in July and August there are lots of church festivals at Cercino dedicated to *La Madonna di Carmine, La Madonna della Pietà* and *La Madonna della Neve* that we can go to."

"Isn't *neve* snow?" I was intrigued. "What's snow got to do with it?"

"You'll find out when we go to Siro for the festival," Michele answered.

On the first Sunday of August, we drove to a small church hidden between a green curtain of trees. Leading me to the side of the chapel where men sat smoking on the low wall, Michele pointed up to an old, gnarled chestnut tree.

"Look up there. Can you see the leaves?"

I followed his finger and saw that the leaves of several branches were white.

"There's a legend that Mary rested on the branches of this tree and ever since, the leaves of those branches turn white during the summer months." I must admit that it felt awesome, being confronted with such a phenomenon with no plausible scientific explanation. It was a veritable mystery.

I just had time for another look before the sound of the bell announced the beginning of the service and, leaving the men outside, the women and children pushed their way into the cramped interior for Mass. Forty minutes later, we trooped out to hear the bartering begin for home-made cakes and bottles of wine. Families chose a place on the rough ground for a picnic, where salami, cold meats, rolls, cheese and wine materialised from bags. Voices filled the warm summer air until it was time for Vespers at 2.30pm. This time, I noticed the hymn sheets were used to fan the sultry air and the singing became more demure. Four men carried the statue of the *Madonna della Neve* up an uneven path and down a steep track. One of the carriers perspired heavily and another almost stumbled over a stone. I understood why several men walked next to them, ready to give a helping hand if necessary. Back at the church, Don Giulio blessed the statue and his parishioners, who in turn gave one last heartfelt rendition of a hymn dedicated to the *Madonna* before it was time for the celebrations to start. Music played, people swirled on the small square dance floor, raffle tickets appeared, and the wine flowed. Laughter and chatter replaced the problems of everyday life for a few hours.

September is a very special month for the Baronas. Michele had already told me in Eastbourne that not only are the grapes harvested, but the 29th is his saint's day, this particular saint also being the patron Saint of the church at Cercino.

"There's a big celebration on the Sunday nearest to the 29th," he said, proudly. Needless to say, on the day before, I woke up to a flurry of movement downstairs. While Carla rattled pans preparing various dishes, Mara swept and cleaned the house.

"Are we too late for breakfast," I whispered to Michele as we walked into the kitchen. I had to get my priorities right.

"Of course not. I need a coffee and something to eat, too," he said with feeling.

I wondered how we could heat the water because something bubbled on each gas ring and I for one, didn't want to invade Carla's territory at that precise moment.

"*Ciao, mam*," Michele guided her away from the gas stove, whispering something in her ear. Then he took a small, steaming pan off and put one filled with water for us, winking at me, while Carla muttered under her breath. Ten minutes later, I joined Mara in the cleaning while Michele joined his father outside for a smoke.

At midday, as the bells rang out through the valley, Mara took out the tablecloth used for special occasions and I laid the table. Meanwhile, Carla brought in a selection of cold meats, pickles and rolls. Lasagne followed, and then a roast joint with a salad. The cheese board came out after that and finally an *espresso*. I wondered how Alberto's little car would take us all up to Cercino. A plate of lasagne on its own would have been enough for me. However, despite the extra weight from such a spread, the Fiat 500 still managed to carry its load.

Both Carla and Alberto, like the rest of the parishioners, dressed up and met outside the church to catch up on the latest gossip and chat to friends and relatives.

The parish church dominates the village and Michele steered me towards the view from the ancient wall surrounding it. At nearly 500 metres from sea level, I could see Lake Como in the distance on my right and villages spreading out like fingers from the base of the mountains. Morbegno lay quietly to my left and the River Adda wound its way through the countryside, sparkling dramatically when the sun reflected on the rippling water. Although I still hadn't become used to the idea that villages existed within the majestic confines of the mountains, now and again the sunlight picked out a car ascending slowly. I inadvertently sighed at the beauty of it but was interrupted by the bells chiming to announce the beginning of Vespers. We dutifully marched into the cool interior of the old church where Don Giulio smiled benignly at the congregation, having had a first class meal with a family who considered him their spiritual son.

Afterwards, we followed the statue of *San Michele* in a procession around the village, not all of us reciting the rosary, but still with heads bowed reverently, chatting about anything except religion. For some reason, I had a great feeling of belonging at such functions and from the beginning everyone welcomed me into the community. A few asked me how the wedding plans were coming along, and wanted to know if I hoped to become a mother as soon as possible. Before I had time to answer, however, Don Giulio came along with an Australian couple. This time I didn't mind Michele talking to his friends, I passed a very pleasant afternoon speaking English to a husband and wife from Adelaide who had come to visit their Italian relatives.

As the wine flowed, the men and women gathered together, regardless of whether they were from Piussogno or Cercino, content to sing their traditional songs of the Valtellina. Their harmonising was pure magic and I was spellbound hearing the locals sing. The rivalry that Michele had so often told me about between Piussogno and Cercino was forgotten on such occasions.

11

Grapes Between the Toes

After the excitement of *San Michele*, the following days seemed dull and empty, the monotony broken only by my initiation to *polenta*. During the colder months, pasta was sometimes substituted by *polenta e spezzatino*. The fire was lit in the corner of the kitchen and a huge, black cauldron-type saucepan was filled with water then hung on a chain just above the flames. I watched fascinated as Carla threw a small quantity of cooking salt into the boiling water before adding yellow flour crushed from the corn cobs. Alberto had the job of stirring the contents continuously with a long, thin wooden stick until it thickened, the whole process taking up to an hour. While Michele's father busied himself with the *polenta*, Carla became a maelstrom of activity as she prepared the meat dish to go with it. This seemed to be a sort of casserole cooked on the gas stove instead of in the oven, except that the preparation time was doubled and it needed constant watching; too time-consuming for my liking.

At the sight of the mound of yellow gunge on a huge wooden platter with a wooden serving spoon stuck in the middle of it, I wondered what excuse I could give to avoid eating it. Before I had time to whisper discretely in Michele's ear, Carla ladled a generous helping onto my plate together with a portion of meat. All eyes focused on me as I gingerly tasted it. To my surprise, I found it fairly edible. You definitely had to acquire a taste for it, but I felt I could get to like it. There was a general murmuring around the table regarding my initial reaction and then it was a case of heads down for the all-important business of eating.

Tedium struck again a few days later and I felt seriously bored and seriously worried. When left to my own devices, I couldn't help but wonder whether I'd ever adapt to village life. I knew I wanted to spend the rest of my life with Michele, but did I want to spend it in Piussogno? The summer festivals had brought some life to the area, as well as English-speaking tourists, but now the summer days were coming to an end and the air had a much cooler edge to it. Going down to breakfast one Saturday morning, I walked into a hive of conversation.

"*Ciao,* we're discussing *La Vendemmia,*" Michele explained.

"*La* what?" I hadn't heard that word until now.

"*La Vendemmia* means 'grape 'arvest' and it's very important for us. Children can even stay 'ome from school. We usually 'arvest the grapes at the end of September, so we're deciding when's the best time to do it."

I found out that in the Barona family there's a ritual for this annual occasion: firstly, the date had to be decided

– weather and business commitments permitting; secondly, according to how many of us would be present in the morning, and who would come in the afternoon, they decided in which order the vines would be harvested. Michele's family had four vineyards dotted around his parents' house, all varying in size. Lastly, they discussed the menu – a most important factor, as there were so many more mouths to feed.

My introduction to grape picking can only be described as a daunting experience. They told me to wear old clothes which made me panic because I didn't own any. I had only been here for two and a half months and I had selected my entire wardrobe to impress my fiancé. Mara came to my rescue, lending me an old pair of trousers and a T-shirt. I decided my comfy shoes would be my best bet to cope with the slippery slopes and uneven walls. Michele gave me a pair of rubber gloves – obviously to protect my varnished nails – a pair of scissors and a knife to cut or snip the grapes. Then, he showed me how to cut the grapes using the scissors.

"Don't try snipping with the knife. You'll 'urt yourself." Such was his faith in my ability.

I tried hard to copy his actions and after watching me for a while and satisfied I wouldn't end up at the local A&E, he went to join Pietro. The vines stood on slopes and several times I found myself balancing on the edge of crumbling walls with two full buckets of precious grapes trying to reach the huge containers where Michele and Pietro waited to empty my contribution. Already hit-or-miss as to whether I could manage to manoeuvre the buckets without knocking them over, I gingerly slid down on my bottom from one vine to the next, picking the grapes nearest to the ground. We worked in pairs, but I made sure I was with Mara. Being the youngest she picked one bunch and ate the next. Sometimes, this involved picking out a few green grapes before putting them in her mouth. If I really concentrated, I could keep up with her pace.

"*Tutto bene?*" Mara asked, while chewing on a mouthful.

"*Sì, sì.*" I replied, believing I was doing incredibly well – all things considered. I shouldn't have spoken so soon. Stretching too far to cut a bunch hidden behind a concrete post, I lost my balance and knocked over the bucket which I'd filled to the brim.

"Nooo!" I screamed, causing all heads to turn in unison.

I watched helplessly as the grapes rolled down the slope in front of me. Seeing the horror on my face, Mara started laughing.

"*Non fa niente.*" She tried to console me by saying it didn't matter, but it did. My pride was hurt more than anything else. I tried to retrieve the grapes on the ground, but had to give up. Instead, I set to work with a vengeance, determined not to let it happen again. Now and again, Mara gestured to me to try some grapes but they tasted quite sour to me.

"They aren't sweet because they're grown for wine." Michele explained.

At the end of my first day of *la vendemmia*, his father proudly gave me a bunch of grapes to taste.

"*Questi sono uva da tavola,*" he said.

128

In other words – table grapes, and therefore sweet. Unfortunately, to me they tasted exactly the same as the ones for wine. I tried desperately to make the appropriate sounds of appreciation – but all I wanted to do was spit them out. I'd have given anything for a pound of seedless grapes from Tesco.

Michele and Pietro had the job of emptying the overflowing buckets of grapes into large plastic containers already on the *motocarro*, a three-wheeler vehicle used for such purposes. The contents were later transferred to the vat. Work stopped at midday for lunch then we continued through the afternoon until 5.30 pm, when we went our separate ways, the women to wash and then prepare the meal, while the men had the job of emptying the grapes into a huge vat stacked at the back of a cellar or something similar. In Michele's case, his father used a small, dark and damp room below the stable where they kept chickens and rabbits. It also doubled as a makeshift garage. To reach the top of the vat, they had to climb a rickety ladder that Michele's father had made.

"You've got to be careful doing this," Michele explained. "A lot of people 'ave died through being overcome by fumes from the wine and 'ave fallen into the vat."

Shivering at the thought, I vowed I'd never let Michele go alone when it was his turn to crush the grapes.

*

"You're going to see something very unusual later on," Michele whispered as he emptied the last of the

129

grapes into the containers. He refused to say anymore, leaving me intrigued, to say the least. We had worked hard over the past two days and now the vineyards looked bare and forlorn. My curiosity grew as I watched the men wash their feet thoroughly and then climb into the vat.

'Surely they're not going to squash the grapes with their feet,' I thought. At that minute, I caught Michele grinning at me and nodding as if he were reading my mind.

"Don't worry, we're only doing this in your honour," he laughed, before adding, "Come and join us."

"*Dai, andiamo!*" Mara was dying to jump in, too. Not one to chicken out, I ran after Mara and washed my feet scrupulously. I rolled the borrowed trousers up as far as possible over my knees and Michele helped me into the wooden vat. The smell of grapes almost overpowered me and I had to catch my breath, but just as quickly a new sensation took its place. The feel of the squishy fruit beneath my feet and the intoxicating atmosphere is something I'll never forget. I felt happily inebriated.

"This is a ritual which 'as almost disappeared," Michele shouted above the squelching and laughter as we each concentrated whole-heartedly on treading the grapes.

"*Oggi giorno, è solo per i turisti.*" His father added. And I understood why it was only a tourist attraction these days.

At the end of our bout in the vat, I admit I was grateful for modern machinery and thankful that

Michele's father had the necessary equipment for processing grapes. I don't think that I would opt to do it more than once.

La vendémmia, a novelty in the beginning, soon proved to be nothing more than hard slog all year round. Each vine had to be grafted on to the old stocks. In the Valtellina the first two branches are pruned, one stem is curved and the other is left straight, ready to be bent over the following year. In spring, when they start to germinate, it's necessary to treat the vines against the various diseases and insects that can destroy them.

For those who were retired, winemaking gave a purpose in life and topic of conversation but for those who had a full time job, it was a different story. The fact that Michele and Pietro had to be on hand all the time to either prune or graft the vines was time-consuming. This laborious manual task had been Michele's father's job until ill health forced him to stop. Even after the harvest, they still had a lot of work to do. The grapes needed to be stored in a wooden vat or *tino* and crushed every morning and evening, for seven days in order to keep the *marc* wet. This also helps to prevent the liquid becoming vinegar instead of wine. The crushed grapes become *must* and as they boil, they let off a gas that can be very dangerous. Michele took me to see how it was done and I held my breath as he climbed up the old, makeshift ladder with several rungs missing, left against the wall. He then used a rudimentary wooden implement similar to a hayfork, to push the grapes down to the bottom.

"The wine gets its colour at this stage." Michele shouted down to me as he pushed as hard as he could but I'm afraid I was too engrossed thinking about the lack of health and safety regulations to take it all in. At this point his father joined us and he continued my lesson on winemaking.

I did my best to look as if this information couldn't have been more exciting for me – and stifled yawns. I kidded myself that in time I would probably feel more enthusiastic about the intricacies of winemaking. For the moment, I couldn't help wondering what would happen when the older generation passed away – would the vineyards around us be dug up and the land sold to property developers? I realised Michele was looking at me.

"Do you make enough wine for all the year?" I asked, feeling I had to feign interest.

"Oh, no," said Michele "We only 'ave bottles for a few months."

I couldn't believe it, all that work for a few measly bottles. In my opinion, it would be so much more sensible to buy local wine but decided to keep those thoughts to myself.

12

Roasted Chestnuts in Autumn

My days followed a pattern: cleaning, shopping, washing and ironing, trying desperately to assume the role of a young Italian woman, squashing all memories of the career-minded English teacher from Poole. As my ability to converse with the natives improved, however, I harboured a thought that maybe one day I could teach English to students. It helped a little to pass the time during disconsolate reflections of what I could be doing with my life; I mean doing housework all day every day can only be described as monotonous. As I fought this inner battle of conflicting thoughts, the weeks passed, the leaves changed from green to their annual autumnal colours and the air became fresher and crisper. Alberto decided to prepare the pipes for the wood-burning stoves which were dismantled after each winter, just in case it suddenly turned colder.

After the grape harvest and the church festival celebrating San Michele in September, the following month of October was dedicated to picking chestnuts. Here again, there is a rule. Only the best chestnuts are used and, Michele whispered, everyone had their own secret place, where only the *biggest* and *sweetest* ones could be found.

Carla informed us one afternoon that she was going to look for chestnuts and asked if we would like to join her. Mara had homework to do and I had to go to Luisa's house for an *extra* Italian lesson – more than anything else it was an excuse to chat to someone my own age – so she set out alone.

When I got back a few hours later, I found everyone in the kitchen admiring her bounty. I truly can't remember ever seeing such huge, shiny chestnuts. They were magnificent.

"*Facciamo le bruciate domani sera,*" Mara announced excitedly. I wondered what she was saying until she pointed to the chestnuts.

The family decided to have *le bruciate* – roasted chestnuts – the following evening when Anna and her boyfriend were coming to see us. The next day, it was Alberto's job to find the *padella per arrostire le castagne,* which had been put away after last year's *bruciate.* I was curious to see what the *padella* was like. He didn't take long to reappear with a very long-handled type of frying pan. It was fairly deep and wide and the bottom had an open criss-cross structure.

"It's a bit old, isn't it?" I couldn't help wondering whether it was time to replace it with a new one.

"It seems very old," Michele explained "but it's just 'ad a lot of use." I tried hard to see the logic in his words but gave up.

Alberto lit the fire in the corner of the kitchen and put

the chestnuts into the pan, leaving them to roast above the flames for about ten minutes, then Michele lifted the pan off and spread cabbage leaves over the top. This stopped them from becoming too hard.

"You can use a wet cloth if you 'aven't got cabbage leaves," Michele explained.

He then lowered the pan down over the ashes and left it for five minutes. Everyone sat around the fire, chatting, all eyes fixed on the *padella.* At last, the pan was ceremoniously laid in the middle of the newspapers spread out on the floor to catch the skin as the chestnuts were eaten. Glasses were handed round of sparkling orange for the women and wine for the men. We then tucked into the sweet chestnuts. I hadn't bargained on them being so hot and squealed as I picked up my very first roasted chestnut. They soon left my fingers black and smudgy and I had to remember not to rub my face. Pushing my hair back from my eyes left me with symmetrical black streaks, which amused everyone around the table.

After the local gossip had been passed on between one chestnut and another, the conversation turned to contraband and how many of the young men in the village and surrounding area had participated at least once during the 1960s and early seventies in an attempt to earn a little extra money. Fascinated, I munched slowly, concentrating on what they said. Apparently, even Pietro had taken part with his cousin and others in smuggling cigarettes and coffee over the border from Switzerland. Their small group had waited until darkness fell before negotiating a mountain pass well away from the border police. One behind the other, they moved silently through the undergrowth cursing under their breath when they trod on broken twigs which creaked under their feet or tripped over gnarled roots of age-old trees. The slightest sound echoed in the blackness, risking an arrest but the booty of cigarettes and coffee awaiting them just across the Swiss border spurred them on. Fascinated, I asked Pietro to continue when he stopped to light a cigarette. He told me that some contrabandists had used their cars in order to get a bigger supply of goods but this involved driving without headlights. He remembered a young man from the village who had lost his life when he crashed his car. Inadvertently, I shivered thinking of the danger it had entailed, glad to know that smuggling nowadays had become history and the paths they had once followed were now nature trails.

The following Saturday, Michele told me that Nino and Emily had invited us for *le bruciate* at their house in Cercino that evening, then a few days later Adriano and Luisa asked us if we'd like to eat *le bruciate*. Italians, I learned, loved to meet up with friends and relatives to eat roasted chestnuts. My introduction to *le bruciate* was a positive one but I couldn't eat half as many as the average Italian consumes. I learnt to camouflage my lack of appetite by talking – and it worked. In theory, you can't talk and eat at the same time, and someone has to direct the conversation – no matter how poor their Italian is.

*

As the autumnal evenings became colder, fires and wood-burning stoves were lit and spirals of smoke oozed out of the chimneys throughout the valley. The old houses didn't have central heating and I was surprised to see that the newly built houses all had a fireplace or an ornamental wood-burning stove as well as radiators.

"Why do they have both?" I was intrigued.

"Central heating is a luxury," Michele told me. "Wood-burning stoves and fireplaces are a necessity."

I nodded slowly as the significance of his words sunk in. I remembered my mum carrying buckets of coal into the house. Over the years, she must have moved tons. Never for one moment did I imagine I'd be lugging equally heavy buckets of logs for five months of the year. I decided not to think about it – that was until Michele announced that he and his brother had to spend the following day with his father chopping down trees on their land and then sawing them into manageable logs to be burnt. Of course, they could only cut the wood when the moon was waning, otherwise it wouldn't burn properly.

"What does that mean? You can only cut wood when the moon's in the right phase?"

"Yes, otherwise it gives off a lot of smoke and 'ardly any flames."

I learnt something new every day. The ritual of preparing wood for the colder months continued until the men decided that enough had been stacked for even the hardest of winters. Alberto complained of the cold while working outside and was exhausted at the end of the day.

"Is it worth all the hassle?" I whispered to Michele after a hard day's work. "Can't they just have radiators put in?"

"Are you kidding?" He couldn't have been more shocked. "*Pà* loves doing it."

"You could have fooled me," I said under my breath. Then as an after-thought: "When we have our own home, will we have central heating?" I crossed my fingers.

"Of course," he smiled. "As well as a fireplace and wood-burning stove."

I should have known.

13

Signora Barona and A Very New Identity

Don Giulio put our marriage bans in the glass case outside the church in the middle of October, a week before we left for Poole. That gave the villagers something to talk about. Michele, a practising Catholic was going abroad to marry the *inglesina*, a Protestant, in an Anglican church. At the time, it was looked upon as a mixed marriage and created a great deal of excitement in the community.

Back in Poole, Mum had to book the church, order the flowers, book the photographer, choose a hotel for the reception and book a room for us for the night. Not to mention deciding on the wedding cake and accommodation for Michele's family. Mum was forever being asked where the bride was and each time she would say: "She's in Italy." Probably through gritted teeth.

The only thing I had to worry about was choosing a wedding dress. This caused great consternation because traditionally, of course, the groom mustn't see the dress until the bride walks up the aisle. But I hadn't mastered the Italian language well enough to explain what style I wanted. Michele and I scoured the local Bridal shops and I revelled in the attention I received every time we entered such a shop. We were talking serious money here and the assistants obviously hoped to make a good sale. Furthermore, it seemed to be a great novelty that we were buying our wedding clothes in Italy to marry in England. Assistants gesticulated in their dramatic way and I learnt phrases such as:

"*Che bello!*"

"*Che romantico!*"

"*Oh, ma che favola!*"

This time, I didn't need a degree in Italian to understand them telling me it was *lovely, romantic,* and like a *fairy tale.* Unfortunately, though, I couldn't find the right dress. I didn't want anything too fancy, or too elaborate, or too revealing but something which mirrored the Italian style, yet something that was me.

"What am I going to do?" I felt tired and disillusioned.

"Look, we 'aven't been to the Wedding Shop in Chiavenna. It's supposed to 'ave a fantastic selection of wedding dresses and suits and it sells everything for the bride and groom on their big day," Michele said optimistically. "And we pass it on the way to Switzerland," he added.

"We'll go tomorrow," I decided.

We arrived at the shop just after 9am and as we opened the shop door, an assistant hurried towards us.

"*Buongiorno. Come posso aiutavi?*"

Michele explained that I wanted a wedding dress.

"*Seguitemi*," she ordered, turning agilely on her stilettos and we obeyed, following her towards rows and rows of beautiful, wedding dresses: white satin, ivory satin, graceful ones with French lacy bodices, elegant gowns with an empire waist. I couldn't help smiling as the assistant asked me to choose some to try on. Having selected the ones that fitted my requirements for the ideal wedding dress, I disappeared into the changing room and Michele settled himself into a strategically positioned chair, ready for a long wait.

I tried on dress after dress until I donned the last but one… and nearly caused the assistant to have a heart attack when I came out of the changing room to show Michele.

"Look. This is just what I wanted. What do you think? Do you like it?"

"No, no." She started waving her arms about. "*Porta sfortuna se lo sposo vede il vestito prima delle nozze!*" She was genuinely worried that it would bring us bad luck.

"It's not a problem for us." I tried to placate her with Michele translating for me when I stumbled over new vocabulary. "We're marrying in an Anglican church in England."

"Oh." She sounded shocked.

"Well, do you like it or not?" I twirled in front of Michele, not sure whether his expression of sheer incredulity was due to the vision of beauty before him or the fact that I'd actually chosen the dress at last. At this point, the owner came out. I can only describe him as *dapper,* very solicitous and, I must add, appreciative of our money being spent in his shop.

Next, we had to choose the wedding rings. We went to one of the local jewellers in Morbegno and once again received preferential treatment. There is an art to flattery and Italians are truly masters when it comes to complimenting customers. Only the hardest of the hard can remain untouched.

As soon as Michele had found an appropriate wedding suit, we booked a flight to England. By ecclesiastical law, we had to stay in Poole for three weeks before marrying which gave us time to meet up with the Vicar to decide on hymns and readings for the service and arrange for the choir to be present. Needless to say, a holiday in Poole didn't go amiss – even though, I must have been the most laidback future bride ever. I certainly wasn't stressed over wedding plans. I'm sorry I couldn't say the same for the *mother* of the bride.

The Barona family drove over later in three cars and Michele's aunt, uncle and godfather came, too. Before coming to Dorset, they visited London and while the aunt changed into her slippers in Oxford Street to ease her aching feet, the rest of the group ignored pinched toes and blisters, absorbed in the splendour of the city. The next day they drove to Poole where Michele and I showed them the wonders of my hometown. Coming to England proved to be some event but, although happy, they also felt tired mentally and physically.

However, the aura of excitement on the day of the wedding quashed all inertia and left them with a palpable sense of energy.

Walking up the aisle on my brother's arm remains a

poignant memory as each step took me nearer to my future husband and a permanent life in Italy. His reassuring hand on mine brushed aside any last minute qualms and the trembling gave way to a feeling of contentment as I joined Michele at the altar.

Unknown to us, the Vicar had been learning some phrases from an Italian woman in the parish and before the wedding ceremony began, he welcomed Michele's family in Italian. It was a lovely gesture and much appreciated. It put them at ease and made them feel part of the congregation. After the ceremony, we had to take our official wedding photos at the hotel because being November the afternoon was cold, wet and windy.

Our reception proved to be a novelty for Michele's family. We had decided on a buffet, totally alien to the Italians: their wedding feasts of up to 16 different courses lasted between five to six hours with a fleet of waiters and waitresses serving the tables. Instead, here they found themselves faced with a self-service meal that only lasted a couple of hours. Jacket Potatoes, in the shape of swans, floored Michele's aunt. Not realizing that she could leave the skin on her plate, she chewed relentlessly on the hard, crisp layer wondering when it would soften, enabling her to swallow. Eventually washing down the last piece with a litre of sparkling water, she saw that everyone else had left theirs behind.

"Hmmm, *buono!*" she said to my grandmother, sitting beside her, who didn't speak a word of Italian.

"Oh, yes, I know." said nanna, smiling happily to *zia*. "It's delicious."

"*Sì, sì!*" agreed *zia*, showing that food has no language barriers.

Michele and I spent our wedding night at the Harbour Heights Hotel and as we looked at the spectacular view of the bay from our window, I tried not to think that it might be a while before I saw the sea again. Sleep eluded me as I thought about our journey back to Italy the following day, until fatigue finally kicked in and I dozed fitfully. Unlike the day before, we woke to a bright, crisp morning with a clear blue sky and after a hearty breakfast, we took a taxi back to Mum's. I finally said goodbye to my family and friends before joining the Italian entourage. Being escorted back to Italy by my in-laws as newly-weds was not what I had had in mind, but I was young and naïve enough to find the situation almost comical. Anyway, we had to forfeit a honeymoon in order to get back to Piussogno as quickly as possible to finish the disco. We maintained we'd take our *Luna di Miele* at a later date...

*

"I can't wait to have my ID card," I told Michele as we made our way to *Il Comune* – the town hall – at Cercino, a few days after we arrived back in Piussogno. I naturally assumed the copy of our marriage licence would be sufficient to enable me to register on the electoral roll and be legally entitled to an Identity Card. Instead, the whole process involved several trips to Cercino where the secretaries weren't always at their desks. Invariably, they were taking their coffee break at the local bar and we would have to wait nearly half an hour before they came back, only to answer some trivial question or sign a form. Now had I been a native, I would probably have joined them for an *espresso* and a chat on these occasions but being English, I found it all very frustrating.

Two requirements for my ID card were three passport photos and a special stamp that could only be bought from certain bars. I had to go to a photographer's to have my picture taken because kiosks where passport photos could be taken still had not reached Morbegno. The photographer actually told me how to pose for the photo; I almost expected a make-up artist to appear.

"*No, no, no! Non guardare così. Girati, sì, sì.*" He moved my head slightly towards him. "*Sì, sì, brava. Sorridi, brava, un bel sorriso. Benissimo!*" He exaggerated his smile to show me just how he wanted it and in the end, I had to smile whether I wanted to or not. The whole situation seemed farcical to me. I then had to take the photos to the *comune* and of course, work was forgotten for the moment while the secretaries made comments about them saying how photogenic I was. The conversation then turned to which parent I took after and so on. There was absolutely no comparison to the way offices were run in England and I decided that if I wanted to keep my sanity it was best if I tried to adapt to the Italian way of life in the Valtellina.

When my ID card finally arrived, my smile froze as I read *Valeria Anna* Baker. I knew women kept their maiden name after marriage but no one had told me that my forenames would have been Italianized on legal documents.

"But this is illegal because I'm not *Valeria Anna*," I argued. Whether Michele was a poor translator or my arguments fell on deaf ears, remains a mystery. After a lot of nodding, gesticulating and sweet smiles from the secretaries, I walked out of the office clutching my new ID card and a new identity. It was bad enough hearing my in-laws call me *Valeria,* which to my ears continued to sound like malaria. An unfortunate coincidence was that the main road going through Piussogno to Morbegno was called *Via Valeriana*. It became a standing joke but for once my sense of humour was sadly lacking.

14

Christmas Trees and Woolly Vests

Nothing had prepared me for the harsh winter months. For the first time in years, I felt the need to wear a vest. As I didn't actually have any, I had to go to Gemma's shop to buy a supply. My mother-in-law told me to buy three: one to wear, one in the wash, and a spare. Considering it was almost a feat in itself to get any clothes dry at all, I could see the sense in having one for an emergency. So one morning in January, after doing the daily shopping, I popped into Gemma's. She busied herself rummaging through cardboard boxes until she found what she was looking for: "*Questa va bene?*"

I was horrified when she showed me a vest that resembled a style from the 19th century. No way could I wear anything like that. I'd rather shiver. She assured me that my mother-in-law and other middle-aged women all bought that type.

"Exactly," I said in Italian, but she didn't catch the irony in my tone.

I asked her if she had anything slightly more modern. She disappeared again before coming back with two different sorts. There wasn't really much to choose between them – both were incredibly unflattering and would have to be worn without Michele seeing me. Still, he had agreed with his mother, when she said that I would soon develop a cold, or worse, if I didn't resort to wearing some serious underwear. I doubt whether even he imagined me in the type of vest that Gemma was now trying to sell me, though. In the end, I chose a sleeveless one and Gemma immediately picked up three. I couldn't make up my mind whether she had already spoken to my mother-in-law or if it really was the norm to buy items in threes.

The following day was a typical, grey winter's day and I happily donned my vest. The cold air had a sharper crispness to it than usual when I set out to do the shopping, yet some of the elderly women only wore a cardigan over a dress and short, hand-knitted socks and clogs. The only sign that they felt a slight chill in the air was the way they tied their headscarves more tightly under their chins and crossed their arms. Instead, I wore a jacket, scarf, and gloves and under my jeans, I had a warm pair of tights and boots. But I still felt chilled to the bone.

"Don't worry. It'll get warmer when it snows." Michele told me cheerfully.

The weather was the general topic of conversation at the shop.

"Yes, snow is definitely on the way."

"Do you think it'll snow as much as last year?"

"Oh, I hope not. It's so difficult to get about when there's a heavy fall." And so it went on.

Back at my in-laws' house, Michele's mum made sure the wood-burning stoves in the lounge and kitchen, the two warmest rooms in the house, were kept alight and a good supply of logs filled a bucket by the side.

With no central heating, my fears were well founded. Sub-zero temperatures meant it was freezing upstairs and nobody spent long in the bathroom. Carla gave me a hot water bottle to give me some warmth in bed. Instead of cosy duvets, we had crisp linen sheets and blankets. A bedspread covered the bed when made, and on exceptionally cold nights, we left it in its place. Any extra layers were well appreciated. Michele suffered tremendously from the cold and his feet were icier than mine. I'm certain I achieved a new world record each time I changed into a pair of pyjamas and jumped into bed. During my introduction to Italian winters, there was no thought given to wearing negligees or skimpy nighties. Oh, no! It was a case of: the more you wear, the better your chances of keeping warm and getting a good night's sleep. I'd have gladly donned bed socks, too, had I owned any.

Then it happened. We woke up to a beautiful snow covered landscape – just like the Christmas card scenes we're so used to sending to friends and relatives. There seemed to be a revered silence all around. As I watched from the window, it started snowing again. I had never seen such huge flakes as the ones falling gently from the leaden, grey skies. The mountains were white, the houses were white, the roads were white. Everywhere I looked, snow had settled. Now and again I could just make out a car driving painfully slowly on the main road below. Snow was great, if you didn't actually have to go anywhere.

Snow meant Michele couldn't go to work, so he decided to come with me to do the shopping. Mara lent me a pair of wellies as there was no way I could walk in the snow with my platform boots. Before going anywhere, Michele had to dig a path down to the gate because already nearly half a metre of snow had fallen. I was surprised to find the air milder as I stepped out into this winter wonderland. It didn't make me catch my breath or leave me with a bright, red nose and freezing ears.

Michele held the umbrella over our heads and guided me with his free arm. He kept telling me to watch where I was walking. I'm sure he had visions of me in hospital with a broken leg. I loved the way the snow crunched beneath my feet. As we passed a field, we heard shrieks of excitement and then Michele's young cousins came into view sliding down the slopes on homemade sledges.

"*Ciao!*" they cried.

"*Ciao!*" we replied, as two of them careered dangerously towards a hedge.

"*State attenti!*" Michele warned, which sent them into fits of laughter as they deliberately fell off and rolled over and over in the snow. We met more children playing on the way. This time, we had to dodge snowballs and I was sorely tempted to join in. Had I been with Mara, I probably would have but with my husband by my side, I decided that on this occasion decorum was necessary.

The older members of the community were pleased that it was snowing at last because temperatures went up a few degrees, but at the same time, they couldn't help muttering under their breaths about the disadvantages it brought; no logs could be chopped up. Nonetheless, the elderly women, enduring the elements with their shopping bag in one hand and umbrella in the other, still wore just their cardigans. How come they didn't end up with pneumonia? The older generation certainly had stronger constitutions. They acknowledged us with a: "*Bondì*", as they plodded by.

Nobody could really understand my enthusiasm at being out in so much snow. Waiting for our turn to be served by Lina, one of the shoppers commented on the look of sheer delight on my face – I mean, it was only snow. With Michele's help, I tried to explain that I had never experienced sub-zero temperatures in my hometown and on the few occasions it had snowed, the snowflakes melted as soon as they touched the ground. Comments followed such as:

"What, you've never seen snow like this before?"

"Don't tell me you've never ever walked knee deep in snow?"

"Well, you'll soon get tired of it, believe you me."

On our way home, we passed the snowplough, clearing the roads. The snowflakes were now thicker and seemed to be falling faster and Michele told me that we wouldn't be going far in the next few days if it continued like this. But, nothing, for the moment, could dampen my enthusiasm for snow.

After two days, however, I changed my opinion, somewhat drastically. I was fed up not being able to go anywhere. If we did venture out, we had to be careful not to slip and it was awkward trying to dry our clothes afterwards. The snow soon turned to slush that tended to freeze dangerously during the night. Walking on black ice was treacherous, to say the least. The council organised a local builder with a bulldozer, which doubled as a snowplough, to help clear the roads as well, and the snow was banked against the sides. At least motorists could now venture onto the roads again – if they were able to reverse out of their drives, that is. Several houses had been built on private land some distance from the main road and access to them was made difficult in such weather conditions. After the snow had been removed, a special lorry sprinkled grit or salt over the tarmac in a vain attempt to prevent black ice forming.

Like the rest of the population, it wasn't long before I was wishing for spring to come along. Snow was great – I decided – when you saw it on a Christmas card.

Talking of Christmas, I had to admit though, as the soft translucent snowflakes tumbled out of a heavy leaden sky, changing the grey world into a shimmering white one, the atmosphere really was magical when it snowed. You could almost imagine Father Christmas on his sleigh.

*

Funnily enough, though, my first Christmas in Italy was

not a white one. Instead, December brought heavy grey skies and the invisible fingers of winter ensured temperatures fell below zero. But despite the cold weather that filtered into your bones, leaving you shivering uncontrollably, it created an air of expectancy that even penetrated the walls of the houses in Piussogno.

Being incredibly busy with the imminent opening of the disco on New Year's Eve, I had little time to feel nostalgic and although I obviously missed my family, I felt quite happy to be with Michele.

His family didn't usually exchange presents but I insisted on buying something for everyone on one of our whistle-stop shopping sprees in Morbegno. Trailing around the shops trying to find inspiration for presents for his family wasn't exactly Michele's idea of fun, but he humoured me.

By mid-November, shop windows were resplendent with their Christmas displays of bunches of holly and fir branches with scarlet bows around them, Father Christmases with overflowing sacks of presents, and gnomes and elves holding out the ideal present to prospective customers who couldn't decide what to give to family or friends. Nearly every shop had a modest fir tree decorated outside the door. A few weeks later, a magnificent Christmas tree appeared in the middle of Morbegno, together with Christmas illuminations strung across the roads, too.

"L'albero di Natale!" Alberto said, grinning as he dragged the Christmas tree into the lounge, totally oblivious to the trail of soil and pine leaves behind him.

He had dug up a small fir tree from the wood behind their house and it had pride of place in the corner, next to the window. We all helped to decorate it with baubles and fairy lights bought from Gemma's shop. I did wonder at the time just how many other people dug up a tree from the woods around us and whether they were replanted afterwards.

At the beginning of December, Christmas trees materialised in the gardens and at night they sparkled spectacularly through the shadows, some with different coloured lights, others in a single shade. Balconies glittered with lights entwined in the railings and those who had a tall tree in the garden put fairy lights around the branches. Towns and villages, like Morbegno, had Christmas lights and decorations hung along the main street, giving off a festive air. To counteract this show of paganism, nativity scenes were everywhere.

"Does everyone make a nativity here?" I asked Michele. I felt a sharp pang of homesickness as I remembered making one each year at home in Poole.

"Certainly, we are a Catholic country," he replied. "Wait till you see the one in Morbegno." He went on to explain that each year, one of the senior schools had the task of making a huge Nativity within a wooden hut.

"It's pretty impressive," I said, when I saw it.

A mill actually worked and a stream ran through the typical biblical scene with statues of figures and animals, while a repertoire of carols played in the background. I thought it would be impossible to better it until Michele took me to see the one at Talamona, a town near

Morbegno. This particular Nativity scene had been set in a dried up river and left me speechless. As we walked over bridges, we found stables housing wooden animals, and almost life-sized figures. Everywhere you looked a trade was depicted and the sounds of the carpenter busily sawing, the women cooking, the miller grinding corn, mingled with the familiar strains of Christmas carols. The Holy Family was the focal point of the entire setting. I suddenly wished my family were with me to share the experience, and once again I felt a tightening in my throat as a wave of nostalgia rose up. Michele's voice broke through my cloud of homesickness.

"Are you ok?" He gently pulled me to him and I felt the sadness slowly fade away as I smiled up into his worried face.

"Yes, I'm fine. I just had a *Baker moment*." This was how I'd come to think of these *down feelings*, I only hoped I wouldn't have too many. He gave me a reassuring hug while we waited for Mara to catch up. On the way out, we passed two men behind a stall selling *vin brulé* (mulled wine) for a reasonable price. Michele bought a cup for me to try but although it certainly warmed me up, I found the cloves made it taste too sweet and strong and so we decided to have a hot chocolate later in a bar in Morbegno.

*

Christmas food shopping that year was an education for me. Carla gave Michele and me a serious shopping list that went on and on. I can honestly say that I had never

155

ever seen such enormous turkeys before. Huge plucked birds sat on rows of trays in the butcher's.

"How many people are coming to eat?" I asked him as we waited our turn

"Oh, only us, I think." 'Impossible', I thought to myself.

As well as one of the massive turkeys, we had to buy an assortment of cold meats, minced meat, salad, tomatoes, *Panettone* (an Italian fruit cake), cheeses, a mixture of nuts, and lastly, fruit. We decided to go to the only supermarket that existed at the time in Morbegno. Pushing our trolley up and down the aisles, I saw that it wasn't just the Baronas doing a *Big Shop*. All the customers seemed to have lists like ours, if not longer. It was a fight to reach the items on the shelves and I had the feeling that we would take more than Michele's predicted half an hour. Another setback was the fact that this Italian supermarket, unlike our English ones, didn't have enough space between the aisles for two trolleys to pass without any trouble. It was much smaller and the narrow spaces involved careful navigating. After crashing into two or three trolleys, and being glared at when I apologised, I handed over to Michele. One consolation for him was that all the men who were out shopping had the same pained expression on their faces. Driving home, I jokingly asked him whether the men helped with cooking preparations but he told me that in Italian households, *only women* spent Christmas Eve preparing the various dishes for the following day.

Watching Carla stir, mix, baste, and boil later that

afternoon, as she moved deftly around the kitchen quite tired me out. With my new status as *Signora Barona*, I wondered whether I should offer to help with the Christmas menu but then decided that I'd only be in the way. Instead, I polished the already gleaming furniture, washed the already clean floors twice and made sure there were enough logs in the box beside the wood-burning stove for the evening, while Michele sat next to his father on the sofa. As I bent to sweep up the ash he'd accidently dropped on the floor, he smiled at me, completely missing the message in the look I gave him. Had he forgotten what ashtrays were for? Nevertheless, I couldn't be cross for long – it was Christmas.

We went to Midnight Mass in the parish church at Cercino on Christmas Eve. Michele told me that Don Giulio had taken the same service at Piussogno at ten o'clock. As we fought for a seat on the hard wooden pews, the priest walked out of the vestry flanked by two altar servers and the congregation started singing the Italian version of 'Silent Night'. I couldn't sing the words but I hummed along happily. Despite the late hour, a lot of children sat fidgeting and I kept hearing the words *Gesù Bambino.* Whereas in England, Father Christmas brings presents to the children, thirty years ago in Italy, it was *Gesù Bambino* or Baby Jesus. The parents tried bribing the children to be good otherwise they wouldn't get any presents from Baby Jesus. On a previous occasion, I had asked Michele if Father Christmas existed for Italian children and he assured me he did. He's known as *Babbo Natale* and the legend is exactly the same.

Christmas Day was literally dedicated to food. Having opened the presents, it was time to get down to the serious business of eating. While Michele's mum busied herself in the kitchen, I couldn't take my eyes off the amount of food sitting on the gas stove, on the kitchen counter and on the small table. I felt sure more guests would turn up. I helped Mara lay the table in the lounge. We used a new tablecloth, the best crockery and polished the glasses that only saw daylight on special occasions. When we took our places, I realised that no one else except the immediate family had been invited. How on earth were we going to eat everything? I didn't fancy a diet of turkey for a week.

We began with cold meats and pickles and Carla brought out her homemade chutney which naturally I was expected to try. It wasn't like my grandmother's which had a very subtle taste to it, but it was good.

The next dish was a generous portion of lasagne. By now I was feeling quite full but, as Michele reminded me, we still had a few more courses to go. There were either second helpings of lasagne or a plate of *ravioli*. Filippo asked me how we celebrated Christmas at home and so I had an excuse to stop eating for a moment in order to explain.

I told them being a small family we had a very modest roast chicken or turkey in comparison to theirs, with stuffing, sausages, roast potatoes, vegetables and gravy. This was followed by Christmas pudding and custard and coffee was served at the end of the meal. (I did my best to define stuffing, gravy, and custard.) My mother-in-law couldn't believe that we ate so little. The equivalent in English of her outburst was: "What? Is that all you eat? But the meal's over before you've even had time to warm the seat!" I went on to explain that in our family, we had Christmas tea later which comprised of trifle, sandwiches, celery, salad and Christmas Cake which was always homemade, as was the Christmas pudding. I tried to describe Christmas crackers, laid at the side of each plate, which we couldn't wait to pull, to find out what prize we had won and then, having read the jokes on the paper strips inside, we all sat with paper hats on our head. Again, this was too English for Michele's family to appreciate. Shaking her head and probably thinking it was a good job her son had chosen to return to his native Italy, Carla disappeared into the kitchen to fetch the roast turkey, along with the vegetables. Thick slices were carved and handed round and everyone tucked in as if they'd just sat down to eat. I surreptitiously slipped some of my meat onto Michele's plate. Bottles of red wine continued to appear and our glasses miraculously remained full to the brim. To my amazement the food gradually disappeared.

When my mother-in-law had decided that no one was going to eat any more meat, she took the remainder into the kitchen, brought back the cheese board and set it in the middle of the table. A bowl of fruit, together with an assortment of nuts followed and Carla insisted I gnawed on a walnut or two. Just as I was wondering how I was ever going to get down from the table, I heard a voice saying: "*Caffè?*"

"*Sì, grazie. Ti posso aiutare?*" I offered to help. The idea of actually doing something physical was too good an opportunity to miss. Together with Mara, I went into the kitchen to make the coffee and it was then that she remembered we hadn't opened the *Panettone*. I suggested we had it later and fortunately, she agreed.

As we drained our coffee cups, a knock at the door announced the first of several visitors and to avoid any more 'sitting and stuffing', I volunteered to wash up which seemed to take forever because of the quantity of plates and cutlery. The fact that we had no constant hot water meant that I had to wait for the water to heat up on the gas stove every time I wanted to change it. Just as I finished washing the last cups, it was time for a cup of tea and a slice of cake and Antonella came to say that if I wanted to call my family from Adriano and Luisa's, we were very welcome to go now. After my last lesson, Luisa had asked me if I'd like to ring my family on Christmas Day and obviously I had said I'd love to. Before that, though, we had to have a slice of *Panettone*. Michele and I then excused ourselves and walked down to their house in the village. The brisk walk was what we needed and really blew the cobwebs away, as my mum used to say.

It was lovely speaking to my family on the phone, despite an unexpected lump in my throat when I heard their voices. After wishing everyone in the Baker household a Merry Christmas, we chatted to Adriano and Luisa before walking down to the disco. Michele put some records on and we listened to music before going back to his parents' house for yet another never-ending six-course dinner. I was sure I'd put on at least three kilos on Christmas Day. How was I ever going to maintain a slim figure when we had such huge meals to contend with? But, if I thought we'd be eating less on Boxing Day, I was wrong. All the shops were closed, so there was more time to spend in the kitchen slaving over a hot stove. I had a nasty feeling that with my aversion to cooking, I was definitely living in the wrong country.

15

A Visit from the Men-in-Black

I had agreed to follow Michele to Italy to be with him and not just his family. So, after a month, not wanting to prolong our forced separation, he gave in his notice at the hotel and came back to Piussogno to work for his father's friend.

At the same time, builders arrived bringing a huge bulldozer that crushed the trees and dug up the soil for the foundations of the discotheque that Michele and his brother planned to open. If it was a difficult moment for their father when he saw his beloved apple orchard become a memory, he didn't show it. To him, his sons were making their dream come true – and that was enough for him. Whereas he was willing to take the risk, his wife was more sceptical. She found it impossible to share the same enthusiasm and was forever speculating over what would happen if it *wasn't* a success and they couldn't pay back the bank loan, building materials or labour. Obviously my inability to comprehend the local dialect helped me to see everything in a positive manner. Even when voices reached decibels higher than the norm, I was blissfully unaware of what was being said.

As this project had started after my arrival, the villagers assumed that I had financed it. People treated me with a new respect and I wallowed in it. I became a real *Signora,* although unfortunately, this didn't happen at 'home' and I had to continue my routine of cleaning the house. Sometimes Pietro let Mara and me help by pouring water into the cement mixer. If it amused the builders when we gave a hand, they never showed it. Occasionally, an old pensioner who considered himself an authority on how to prepare cement joined us. He took his stance near the cement mixer and then, hands in his pockets, cigarette firmly between his teeth, he instructed us on the exact quantity of water and cement.

"Mettete più acqua, più acqua." He'd tell us to pour in more water.

After a while we didn't take him too seriously because most of the time there was only water sloshing around inside. I loved watching him talk without losing his cigarette. I had never smoked but I was sure I would find it a physical impossibility to balance one between my lips and talk at the same time as he did.

The builders worked relentlessly never adhering to such trivialities as a tea or coffee break. I couldn't help wondering how a British builder would react to this work regime. As the walls grew, one by one, the villagers came to view the building. Very few of the older people understood what a disco was. Some knew that their grandchildren went to dance in such places at weekends but they had no idea what a disco looked like inside. A few thought it must be something decadent. This particular group watched the builders at work for a while before walking away slowly, shaking their heads and tutting. Others seemed genuinely intrigued:

"Can we see what it's like when it's finished?"

Pietro promised them a *cappuccino*, if they didn't want anything stronger.

Before they finished the walls, the builders asked me whether I wanted to have the honour of cementing a brick in place.

"I'd, um, love to." I stammered.

Too proud to admit to a fear of heights, I clambered up the scaffolding as if I did it on a daily basis. My hands shook as I took the heavy, red brick and covered one side of it with cement, hoping that it would be interpreted as deep emotion and not sheer terror. With a flourish I put it in place then handed the spatula back to the builder. If he read the panic in my eyes, he didn't acknowledge it and I will be forever grateful to him. No way did I want to give the impression of being weak in any circumstance.

An articulated lorry with a special escort delivering the huge cement pieces for the roof caused quite a commotion in our sleepy village and again, the inhabitants turned up to see what was happening. One afternoon, I noticed a super-sleek, black car swish by, slowing up as it passed the budding disco. It was an incongruous sight in the village and I wondered whether its owners had driven up from Milan for the weekend. No one else commented on it – they were all too busy discussing the disco.

The entire construction materialised before my eyes in three months and the day the builders finished the exterior, they put a branch on the roof.

"It's a tradition 'ere," Michele explained. "A branch put in the chimney or on a roof, shows the building is finished and everyone goes out for a meal to celebrate. We'll 'ave to book a table for twenty at a local restaurant."

'Any excuse for a binge,' I thought to myself.

They aimed to open for Christmas which was ambitious even by my standards. As soon as the plaster finished, the electrician came to fix the wiring. He walked as if he suffered continually from small electric shocks.

"It's probably due to the accident 'e 'ad several years ago, when he fell from the church ceiling while repairing a light." I'm afraid I couldn't help but smile when Michele told me that Giacomo had had a narrow escape and *someone* must have been looking after him. Everyone was so used to seeing him walk that way that they thought nothing of it. I wondered if he should be expected to climb to the top of the ceiling of the disco to fix the lighting but apart from his strange gait, he seemed professional enough. So, sending up a silent prayer, I moved my attention to more pressing affairs: trying to imagine what the disco would look like on the opening night.

The plumber knew both Michele and Pietro well and a lot of banter went on between the men. He drove a *Piaggio Ape* – a small, characteristically Italian tricycle pickup truck – and always dressed in blue dungarees which made him seem bigger than he was. He offered to give me a lift one afternoon to the shop in Piussogno. The perfect gentleman, he opened the door for me and then slammed it shut with such force that I winced. With English cars you had to gently pull them to you or at least, in my family's case. It seemed the most unreliable source of transport ever invented. As he turned the key in the ignition, the *Ape* spluttered to life and vibrations pulsed through the seat from the engine. I felt every stone as we bounced over the uneven ground leading down to the main road. Thankfully, the noise of the motor made any conversation impossible and so, clutching my bag, I tried not to fall off the seat.

Italians are diligent workers, except when there is a problem concerning *health*. The tiler had nearly finished laying the tiles when his back started playing-up.

"Ahia!" A painful cry echoed from where he was working. I ran to see what had happened and found him trying to ease himself into a standing position. He clutched his back with one hand while the other clasped his forehead. He groaned with each movement and had to be helped out to the car and driven home.

"'E's always suffered from back problems," explained Michele.

"Not exactly the ideal job, if that's the case, is it?" I couldn't help adding.

A week passed and he still hadn't shown up for work and until the floors were tiled we couldn't continue with other jobs. When Michele finally managed to speak to him, he told him he had to finish the injections his doctor had prescribed for the pain before he could lay the last few square metres. Hopefully, he'd be back at work the following week. Instead of feeling frustrated – like me – Michele and his brother accepted this as just another *small* problem. In the meantime, the plumber and the electrician did what they could and the disco walls were painted, while Michele and Pietro finally decided on a raised circular dance floor made from a type of aluminium that reflected the lighting above it. They designed the DJ's corner very carefully because it was to be the first disco in the Valtellina with a DJ. The other discos in the area had live music. Both Michele and Pietro had been impressed with the type of discos they'd seen in England and Germany but wanted theirs to be special. Another friend laid the burgundy carpet on the raised areas around the dance floor.

"I 'aven't seen him since we went to school and I remember he 'ad a terrible stammer," Michele told me later.

"Well, there's no sign of a speech impediment now. I thought that we are good talkers, but he could beat me any day." And I meant it. He worked almost as quickly as he talked so he didn't take long to do the job.

The day the technicians finished the dance floor and the speakers had been installed, we held our breath as Michele switched on the central ball light. Tiny fragments of rainbow colours danced on the shiny, metal surface below as it turned slowly. Choosing a record to test the acoustics, we found ourselves gyrating to the rhythm on the circular dance floor. Fantastic!

Now we had to wait for the chairs and tables to be delivered. Whereas in England everything has to be done *yesterday*, and usually goods are delivered on time, here you have to wait at least a couple of weeks, if not longer, and there is always a plausible excuse for the delay. It's a way of life – and one that only Italians can adhere to – but suddenly, everything came together. After putting our heads together, trying to think of an original name for the disco, Michele and Pietro decided to call it the Rendez Vous because that is exactly what it would be: a meeting place for young people.

A commission came to check that the Health and Safety Regulations had been respected – and passed it second time round. Before we realised, it was the middle of December and we had to get ready for the grand opening.

"I've never seen you so excited before," I told Michele.

"It's because my dream is coming true," he smiled back.

One afternoon, Michele was sorting through records, Pietro had gone to Morbegno and I was polishing the tables, when I heard voices. Wanting to know who they belonged to, I stopped what I was doing and started to walk towards the foyer.

Three men in expensive, dark suits and each wearing dark glasses, strode up to the bar.

'This is like a scene from *The Godfather*,' I felt a terrible urge to laugh. I half expected one of the men to produce a violin case containing a rifle. At this point, I decided it might be to my advantage to stay where I was and continue polishing. Not that my vivid imagination had got the better of me or anything.

Michele acknowledged the newcomers and offered them a drink. After a while, Pietro arrived and joined the group. Curiosity got the better of me and I moved closer to get a better view. The conversation became quite animated at times and I noticed that both Michele and Pietro shook their heads repeatedly. One man pointed towards the dance floor and I caught a glimpse of gold cufflinks flashing on a crisp white cuff. I automatically ducked behind a chair, feeling my spine tingling with a mixture of fear and excitement. Creeping closer and closer within the labyrinth of chairs and tables, I could see the expensive watches and elaborate gold bracelets on their wrists as they gestured to enforce their views. They exuded wealth and at the same time an element of danger. Eventually, the three men-in-black left. Moving quickly and silently, I tiptoed out to the foyer and quietly opened the door just in time to see a shiny, black Mercedes purr down to the bottom of the road. Could it have been the car I'd seen the other day? Michele and Pietro still had their heads together, talking in dialect and weren't even aware of my presence until I tapped Michele on the shoulder. He jumped, which was totally out of character.

"Have we just had a visit from the local mafia?" I asked, jokingly, expecting them to laugh – only they didn't.

"They're from somewhere near Lake Como and came specifically to ask if we wanted to pay them *protection money.*" Michele replied without any preamble.

"And…?"

"And we refused their *kind offer* but now we 'ave to be careful nothing 'appens to the disco… or us."

"Oh." As the significance of what Michele said sunk in, I realised that this was for real.

We decided to take turns to sleep in the disco at night, just in case *something* happened. Nobody wanted to actually voice what that *something* could be. I was well aware of the fact that we were taking a risk by spending the night there, but at the same time there was a certain quantum of suspense.

"What if someone tries to set fire to the disco? Or someone tries to break in? What can we do? We'll put up a fight – of course, won't we?" Yes, despite my 22 years I was still incredibly naïve. But, if Michele felt anxious, he didn't show it. The two of us decided to be on guard duty that evening and armed with no more than pillows, blankets and torches, we prepared to sleep. What a joke. I soon found out that I wasn't as brave as I'd thought. Every sound made me jump.

"Is that a car coming here?" I nudged Michele awake.

"Did you hear that creak? I'm sure someone's trying to get in."

"That dog barking means there's trouble ahead."

Michele didn't know whether to laugh or cry. In the end, he told me to shut up and go to sleep. I wasn't used to being told what to do, but I must have been tired because I dozed off. The next thing I knew light was flooding through the disco and Michele was handing me a cappuccino and a brioche. We had survived the first night without any traumas – apart from the ones I'd created, that is. We walked home to change in silence, immersed in our own thoughts of what might or could happen to the disco.

The local police couldn't help us because we had no proof that these men had ever set foot in our place. We had no names, no car number plate, nothing. The police assured us that should anything happen, the disco's alarm would alert them at the police station and, providing there were two available policemen, they would come immediately. Small consolation – and if there weren't two available policemen, what happened then? I dreaded to think. We were left to our own devices.

The following evening, Pietro kept vigil together with his sister and her boyfriend. It was the days before mobile phones and the landline was in the office, situated to the right of the foyer – not the easiest of places to get to in an emergency. We continued our vigilance for a week, then, as there had been no mishaps, decided to stop for Christmas.

The opening night drew nearer and we focused all our energies on making it a success, deliberately pushing all negative thoughts of *mafioso* infiltrators who could easily cause havoc, to the back of our minds.

Bottles of champagne and *Panettone* and *Bisciola* cakes were ordered to be served at each table. Cousins and friends were called on to help serve. There was a great feeling of excitement all round. Where I was concerned, it was also a case of what I should wear and how I should style my hair. I mean, I was the owner's wife and everyone knew I was English. I wanted to make a good impression.

Before we knew it, the day arrived and apprehension and trepidation replaced the excitement we'd all felt up to then.

"What if we get another visit from the Men-in-Black when the disco's open?" I didn't want to dampen Michele's enthusiasm but I couldn't help being anxious.

"I'm sure they won't come when there are lots of people – they're far too subtle for that." His excitement thwarted any other emotion.

Nobody had much of an appetite that evening, so we decided to go to the disco early. The DJ arrived soon after us and immediately started playing the hits of the moment. One by one the people employed for the opening night walked in and awaited instructions. I took my place behind the counter in the foyer and adjusted the blocks of tickets ready to hand out after the entrance fee had been paid, allowing each person a free drink at the bar. Michele's cousin joined me. She was to help hang up coats and give me a hand if there was a sudden rush.

"*E se non viene nessuno?*" One of the cousins quipped. A lot of money had been spent on publicising the opening of the disco with posters everywhere you looked, but even so, there remained the possibility that it might not be the success we had hoped for.

"Well, in my opinion," I said aloud without thinking, "Michele and Pietro have enough relatives to fill the disco." Everyone laughed, nervously.

We needn't have worried. By eight that evening, half an hour before opening time, there was already a queue of people waiting for the doors to open. Two hours later, the car park was packed and cars were parking at the side of the roads leading up to the Rendez Vous. Most of the young people came from our area and we knew them well.

I was surprised by the fact that not many had dressed up for the occasion. The majority of girls were wearing jeans and jumpers, albeit designer ones. Those who *had* made an effort with their appearance looked as if they'd just stepped out of the front page of *Vogue*.

I worked non-stop for the first couple of hours with an endless stream of people, pushing and shoving, trying to beat their friends to the counter. The word *queue* just didn't exist in their vocabulary. Now and again, Michele's dad would appear behind me to count the cash I'd accumulated from the entrance fee. None of us had ever seen so much money before. When there was a lull in people coming in, I managed to take a look at the disco in full swing. The dance floor was packed. I was sorely tempted to forget my place in the entrance and join them. It was New Year's Eve and as we neared the end of 1977, the DJ counted the last seconds to midnight and a New Year. There was a chorus of "*Auguri di Buon Anno*" while outside, the church bells tolled midnight. Cakes and champagne were served at every table which came as an unexpected surprise to their occupants. The disco closed at one in the morning and as the dancers trooped out, they all said, "*Ci vediamo domani*". (See you tomorrow.) We were euphoric. No way could we have anticipated such a fantastic first night.

"And we didn't have any unwanted guests." I whispered to Michele as we closed the doors.

"Right then, let's start clearing up and washing glasses," Pietro said rubbing his hands together.

After a half-hearted effort, we decided to do the job properly the following morning. The first night had been a success. The Rendez Vous opened Sunday afternoon and again in the evening. Michele's dad had never seen or handled so much money before and he had the all-important job of looking after it. He later confided to us that he'd slept with Saturday's takings under his mattress.

Sunday afternoon found us crossing our fingers for a second time, hoping to fill the Rendez Vous again. We worried unnecessarily – the queue started half an hour before we opened and there was a steady flow of young people all afternoon wanting to dance in a disco with a DJ. The evening session was the same, except for the appearance of two distinguished men who paid for their tickets from a fat wad of notes. Fear shot through my body like a torpedo. 'Are you who I think you are?' I wondered. Asking Lella to take over, I quickly made my way inside to find Michele.

"Have you seen them? What do think they're doing here?"

"Who?" Michele had no idea what I was wittering on about.

"The two well-dressed men who just came in. Do you think they've been sent by the three *mafiosi*?"

Michele started laughing.

"If you're referring to the men over there talking to

Pietro, then you've nothing to worry about. They're the owners of a restaurant by Lake Como." Giving me a reassuring hug, he moved towards the group and I slunk back to work. I made a mental note to curb my imagination.

The following weekend, people actually had to be refused admittance. According to the Health and Safety Regulations, we could only take 800 people, and that number had been reached halfway through the evening. I could keep track by the amount of tickets I'd sold. Several groups waited outside until some of the younger generation had to go home, allowing them to take their place on the dance floor. Before long, people drove from Milan and even Switzerland to enjoy the experience of our disco.

On one occasion, a group of Arabs from Saudi Arabia arrived. They spoke English and I was more than happy to chat to them in my own language. They were travelling around Europe and had come to Milan, the capital of fashion, to buy designer suits. Hearing about a new disco called the Rendez Vous, in the Valtellina they joined a crowd of *Milanesi* to come and see it for themselves. I introduced them to Michele, stressing the fact that he was my husband, after I got the impression that one Arab in particular was becoming a little too attentive, especially when he invited me to return to his country with him, telling me he'd buy me jewels, clothes, a big house, everything I wanted. When they went inside once more to dance, or so I thought, I breathed a sigh of relief. Instead, the one paying me compliments had gone to look for Michele in order to ask him how much he wanted for me. He intended taking me back to Riyadh as another member of his *Harem*. Fortunately for me, Michele was adamant that I was not for sale and after a while, they said goodbye and left. When we were on our own, he jokingly admitted he had been tempted but the offer hadn't been high enough. This subsequently became a bone of contention between us every time we had an argument; Michele wishing he'd accepted the offer to sell me and me wishing I'd accepted the offer of a life of luxury.

After a few months, several older couples approached Michele and Pietro to ask them if they would consider opening the disco on a Friday night, specifically for *Liscio* dancing, the equivalent to Old Time Dancing. Having discussed it they decided to give it a go and we were surprised at how many young people turned up, too. We now opened three days a week.

The Rendez Vous proved to be an overwhelming success and one day a letter came through the post saying that we had won a special award for being the first disco in the area. Michele and Pietro had to go to a well-known disco in Milan to receive a cup from a young comedian. It also lived up to its name and several of our friends found their future partners on the dance floor or at the bar.

16

Just the Two of Us

I'm sure it was a foregone conclusion to the family that Michele and I would be a permanent fixture at number 18 but as a newly married *English* bride this didn't fit into my plans. I had other ideas; I had married an Italian but I was still very English in my outlook on our life together. One major drawback living with the family was the fact that there was always someone vying for Michele's attention.

Thanks to the success of the Rendez Vous, the economic factor meant that Michele could give up the building job he had been doing and work full time on the disco and I happily thought I would spend more quality time with him – alone. Unfortunately, it didn't turn out like that. Wherever we went, one of his family came, too. A kernel of resentment started to form and I felt less tolerant towards them, and, in fact, I'm sorry to say that at times I positively bristled. Married life in Piussogno didn't mean *just the two of us*.

On one of the rare occasions we found ourselves alone, I suggested that it might be a good idea if we looked for a flat of our own. Surprisingly, Michele quickly agreed, but warned me that it could be difficult to find one. This was the Valtellina, twenty years behind the rest of Europe, but I was optimistic. If I wanted to celebrate our first wedding anniversary, I had to be.

My mother-in-law was shocked when she heard we wanted to move out. Why couldn't we just build another room upstairs and stay there?

I found it hard to get used to the concept of Italian families living at home all together until they married and then moving into the flat upstairs. I made a mental note to choose a bungalow – if and when – we ever had a place of our own.

I didn't mind where we went to live, as long as we could be alone together.

We heard about an available flat in Piussogno. *Signor* Luigi Gusmeroli, a large, friendly man who made a living as a long-distance lorry driver and his wife, Nanda, who was kept busy looking after their two children, seven year-old Sofia and five year-old Luca, lived in a big, two-storey house and there was a flat available in it. She was glad to know she would have company when her husband was away. Luigi told Michele to go and have a look at the top floor flat and if it was what we were looking for, we could move in straightaway. They gave us a tour of our flat-to-be: a kitchen, lounge, bathroom, and three bedrooms. All the rooms were spacious without being too big. It was just what we were looking for. Then they showed us their flat below. Considering they had two young children, the rooms were spotless;

no toys scattered about or books thrown on chairs, everything was in its place and the floors literally shone. I wondered whether I'd be so meticulous. They were really nice people and we didn't think twice about signing a contract between us for two years.

Thanks to Adriano and Luisa, we heard about a second-hand kitchen for sale and went to see it. It had hardly been used and was in excellent condition – so, we bought it. Then we went to the furniture shop in Piussogno to look at bedrooms. Italian furniture is, and always will be, very expensive due to the lavish way it is made. Naturally, I happened to choose the most expensive bedroom suite they had on display. While the shop owner smiled happily at my impeccable choice, Michele groaned at the thought of the hole in our bank account. I have to confess that I was disappointed at having a double bed that comprised two single metal frames inside the chic, wooden framework and two single mattresses, after all I'd said. Somehow I managed to succumb to the well-rehearsed shoptalk as to why we should buy such a bed. Not only was it apparently more comfortable, it was also easier to lift off single mattresses and pull out single frames when cleaning, something which I hadn't considered until then. At least the bed and accessories were brand new.

For the time being, we decided to forgo the idea of furnishing the lounge. It was enough to have the kitchen with a table and six chairs, and our bedroom. We had no intention of entertaining in the immediate future.

The people who owned the furniture shop – a family

concern – delivered the bedroom suite and there was great discussion as to where to put the bed because for some reason that eluded me, it was imperative that we slept facing north.

"*Non puoi mettere il letto qui,*" they told me categorically.

Why couldn't I have the bed where I wanted it?

"*Tutti sanno che bisogna dormire verso il nord.*"

I must have been the only person who didn't know you had to sleep facing north but to be truthful, I couldn't have cared less where the bed was positioned, so long as we were in our own flat, in our own bedroom, on our own. They put up the kitchen cabinets for us, too, which I dutifully washed and dried and wedding gifts of plates, dishes, glasses, cups and saucers were stacked away. Mara took great delight in helping me, chattering non-stop, not even waiting for a reply.

Sofia and Luca would pop up to see us as soon as their mother was busy with some chore and too absorbed to wonder where her children had got to. When she became aware that they were missing, she would belt out their names and with a hurried: "*Ciao*", they disappeared downstairs. Sofia was a pretty girl with dark, curly hair and big, brown eyes, a typical *bambina,* playing with her dolls and helping her mother. She was polite and quiet, too. Her brother, Luca was the exact opposite. Although he had the same colouring as his sister, that's as far as any resemblance went. He had a cheeky expression and was always up to mischief. Our first introduction to Luca was when we went to negotiate terms for the flat with his parents. As they opened the gate for us a small boy appeared from nowhere and asked: "*Hai una cicca?*"

"*No, mi dispiace. Non ne ho.*" Michele looked sheepish at not being able to give him any chewing gum. His mother gave him a clip round the ear and told him to make himself scarce, while they ushered us into their house.

The day we moved in, I noticed a lot of curtain waving and despite it being a cold day in February, several families remembered jobs that needed doing urgently in the garden, to ensure them a prime view of what was going on.

Michele and I drove backwards and forwards in his dad's Fiat 500, packed with all our worldly goods. He had generously lent it to us until we could buy a car of our own. It seemed to take forever but by late afternoon, we'd finished. I plugged in my loyal radio from my student days and with the music to help me, worked hard, singing away at the same time.

We had already installed the wood-burning stove in the corner of the kitchen; so it was just a question of lighting it and putting the food away. I left Michele to his own devices while I finished the kitchen and then tackled the lounge, a large, bright room with a balcony. Our furniture consisted of tables and chairs left over from the disco and an old 'zed bed' with an even older mattress that acted as a sofa. With a throw-over on it and a few colourful cushions I'd bought at Morbegno market, the lounge took on a very bohemian look.

Our age dictated our priorities; instead of buying

curtains or rugs or lampshades, our main concern was to have a television. This had been one of the first things we'd bought when we signed the contract for the flat and were given the keys. It now had pride of place on a table in the corner of the lounge and we were delighted with it. Our lampshades, for the moment, were Chinese paper lanterns from Woolworth's, sent by my sister. The bathroom was blue, a fashionable hue at that time, but a very cold colour to me. Never mind, it was ours. My hand almost shook with excitement as I put our toothbrushes in the holder along with the toothpaste of my choice. I'd also bought new towels that only we would use as well as my favourite soap. Michele helped me make the bed and put his clothes in the drawers of our brand new chic Italian bedroom suite, before sneaking off to curl up on the sofa to watch telly. I decided to finish the bedroom the next day, when the DJ on the radio said it was nearly 6.00pm

Michele's mum had wanted us to eat with them that evening, but I'd politely refused. I wanted to have our meal in our flat and I'd already decided on the menu – I'd taken it from a recipe book given to me by my school friends for my 18th birthday. The *Love Is* cookbook offered simple and easy dishes to prepare. While making our first meal, I felt happier than I'd been in a long time. An hour later it was nearly ready and I set about laying the table. As I put down the plates and glasses, I remembered that we didn't have any cutlery. Anna and Filippo had promised to give us a cutlery set as a wedding present but they still hadn't got round to buying it. Italians are born with an innate amount of patience – which I still had to acquire. Being too proud to let my mother-in-law know I'd forgotten, I slipped out of the flat and ran to my ex-teacher's house. Luisa opened the door as soon as I rang the bell and if she was surprised to see me standing there, out of breath, she didn't show it.

"*Ciao!* Sorry to bother you, but we've just moved into number twenty-two, and I thought I'd remembered to buy everything we needed, only..." In my stuttering Italian, I went on to explain that I'd prepared a special dinner for Michele but we could only eat it with wooden serving spoons.

"No problem." She gave a quick nod and disappeared, returning a few minutes later with two knives, two forks, two spoons and two teaspoons. I thanked her, saying I'd bring them back the next day, then ran home as fast as I could. Fortunately, Michele was so engrossed watching the documentary on television that he was unaware of the drama in the kitchen. I waited until we had nearly finished eating before telling him what had happened. Not that it really mattered – we'd have used our fingers. Nor was I sure if my culinary effort that first evening was really as appetizing as we both made it out to be or whether we were just euphoric to be on our own. All I know is that I was very proud of my homemade vegetable soup, followed by 'egg surprise' in a bread roll, fruit salad (with the compliments of Del Monte) and coffee to finish. Okay, so I still had a lot to learn where cooking was concerned but then, Michele hadn't married me for my mouth-watering menus.

The first morning in our flat was sheer bliss. We both got up when we wanted to, without any preliminary whistles or raised voices from downstairs to assure we were awake. I padded into the bathroom without having to queue and deliberately took my time. The fact that I could use a dry towel for once was worth the rent to me. Michele and I shared a silent but companionable breakfast – I was never one to make conversation over my cereal, then Michele left to go to the disco to meet a rep and I walked down with him to the shop. True to my word, I opted for the grocer's on the main road. When I walked in, there was quite a bit of nodding and muttering among the customers already waiting to be served. Obviously, word had got round that we had moved out and I was doing my own shopping. For the villagers, it was difficult to understand why I had wanted to leave my in-laws' house. Their motto seemed to be 'the more, the merrier'. The fact that I had no family here made it all the more mystifying why I preferred to stay on my own with Michele. Surely it was better to stay with my husband's family and have lots of company and people to talk to. I kept my eyes firmly fixed on my list to avoid any physical or verbal contact and waited patiently for my turn.

"Buongiorno, come posso aiutarla?" Giovanna tactfully asked what I needed before bustling around collecting the items as quickly as possible. When she didn't understand what I had said, she simply asked me to repeat it, pretending she'd forgotten. I soon understood what "... *e poi* ...? " meant (and then?) For the time being, I decided to pay for the shopping on a daily basis as

opposed to having a little blue book like everyone else.

Counting out the lire, I thanked her as she handed over the bag and she complimented me on how well I had learnt to use the Italian currency. We exchanged a few pleasantries, just to prove to the customers that my Italian was improving, then with a: "*Salve a tutti.*" I waltzed out of the shop. I had heard this phrase a lot and had been dying to use it. Hopefully, I'd pronounced it correctly.

*

Back home, I set about putting the last of the clothes away in the bedroom, before giving the furniture a good polish. Before I knew it, it was time to get lunch ready. As the bells tolled midday Michele walked in, sure to find his plate of pasta on the table. Both my grandmothers had given me some very sound advice: "Whatever you do, always have the cloth on the table at mealtimes. Even if it's not quite ready, it looks as if it won't be long..." I had remembered to put out the rolls, cold meats and cheese, too. Something edible made it look good. *Pasta al dente* was the correct way to serve any pasta dish, but mine tended to have an over-cooked aura about it in the beginning.

Béchamel sauces were definitely not on my menu for the time being, either. I decided to stick to simple recipes that were impossible to go wrong. Unlike most newly married husbands, Michele was one who did not put on weight. I preferred not to ask myself whether it was due to our plain diet or my love of cooking which was sadly lacking. My mother-in-law soon noticed that her son was not filling out as was the norm, and decided to invite us for a meal of *polenta e spezzatino* at least once a week.

*

My new life fell into a regular pattern: shopping and housework in the morning, before walking down to the disco with Michele in the afternoon. I still hoped to find a job in a local language school teaching English but my teacher's certificate wasn't recognised in Italy. Again it was suggested by one apologetic principal that I enrolled at university to study languages, after which, with an Italian/English degree I could probably find a job in a school. Naturally, I refused to even consider this alternative. Instead, I threw myself wholeheartedly into the serious role of wife and housewife, keeping our flat neat and tidy. Sometimes I would have a chat to Nanda in the garden while the children were at school, sitting on one of the patio chairs or benches that nearly all Italian gardens had. She had trained as a dressmaker and showed me the correct way to hem a piece of clothing.

Very often, on a fine windy day, I would see mattresses and bed linen hanging out of windows as I walked to the shop. Nanda, too, aired her bedding on a regular basis. When I asked Michele the reason for these displays of *bed touting*, he explained that it was considered hygienic to give the beds an airing.

"Am I expected to do it, too?" Rather a stupid question, in the circumstances.

"If you want to 'ave a 'ealthy night's sleep, yes."

The next time I decided that the weather conditions were favourable for exposing our mattresses and sheets to the elements, I dragged the two heavy, single mattresses one at a time, and balanced them over the windowsill, before going back for the rest of the paraphernalia. As I turned round with the bundle in my arms, I realised that the mattresses had disappeared. I had a nasty feeling that perhaps I'd been a bit too enthusiastic in practically throwing them out of the window instead of propping them over the sill. Peering down into the garden below, I saw them, one on top of the other. No way could I lug them up two flights of steps, so I had to wait for Michele. He was not amused by my first attempt at imitating Italian housewives, but I assured him that it wouldn't happen again. Unfortunately, it did. At this point, Michele suggested that I aired everything – within the bedroom. I was lucky that Nanda was busy both times and didn't see what was going on upstairs.

*

Once or twice I had people coming to the door asking me to translate instructions for various electrical appliances written in English or letters from long-distance relatives who wanted to keep in touch with their Italian family. The latter were either scribbled notes from elderly relations who could no longer remember dialect and had forgotten their native language, or handwritten pages of news from younger family members who had solemnly promised their elders never to forget Italy. When such visitors presented themselves, I would invite them in and offer them a coffee or a cold drink before getting down to the business of translating. Often I had to write the Italian version for them in case they forgot. The women couldn't help but look curiously at how I had furnished the flat.

"Hmm. It's nicely furnished," they'd say in dialect, having a good look around. It was hard to accept their candid curiosity for anything but nosiness.

"They're just interested in 'ow an English girl 'as set up 'ome," Michele assured me. I wasn't convinced. It occurred to me that some might have used the excuse of having a short-term memory to stay longer and take in as much as they could.

Other regular visitors were the immediate family. They usually rang the bell when I had just finished washing up after the evening meal. I wondered, irreverently, whether it was my mother-in-law's way of making sure I actually cooked for her son. I mean, if I had given him a steak you could smell the meat.

Michele's aunt, who lived just a few doors away from us, took to popping in. I enjoyed her visits because her cheerful disposition and sense of humour made a welcome change from the serious outlook of life most of the villagers shared.

On one occasion she turned up while I was in the middle of making a beef casserole and was peeling onions with tears streaming down my face. Without thinking I opened the door, sniffing in a very unladylike manner at the same time.

"Oh, *mamma mia. Cosa c'è?*" She asked, patting me on the shoulder. She was convinced I was having an attack of nostalgia and when I laughed through my tears, she thought I was just being brave. Only when I led her into the kitchen and showed her the onion slices did she believe me. She then went on to explain that putting onions under cold water beforehand helps to stop eyes running when peeling them.

Another time she caught me furiously hunting for some photos I'd just collected. I couldn't remember for the life of me where I'd put them.

"Ah, " she said, prophetically, "*La casa nasconde, ma non ruba!*"

'It's true,' I thought, 'the house *hides* things, but it doesn't *steal*.' *Zia* proved to be a fount of such sayings and always reminded me so much of my maternal grandmother. Apart from the obvious age difference, and despite a basic education, they both had wisdom beyond words and I loved them dearly.

During the evenings when our visitors had gone, we curled up in front of the television. I couldn't believe my eyes when I saw they were televising 'Poldark'. Scenes of the Cornish coast and countryside made me feel a bit nearer to home. The dubbing was excellent, too. One criticism I had of Italian television though was the number of scantily dressed females on quiz shows and adverts.

"Is it a tactic to distract the contestants?" I asked. Michele was too busy drooling over a bikini-clad female to answer and was totally unaware of the cushion flying through the air until it found its target. Smiling to no one in particular, he laid it beside him on the sofa, made himself comfy again and returned his attention to the screen. Men!

*

"I think it's time we gave *pà* back 'is car and started looking for one for us," Michele announced one lunchtime. 'Goodness,' I thought, 'first our own flat and now our own car.' Thanks to Filippo, we found a second-hand Fiat 600. It was just the right size for me, small and easy to park and its canary yellow colour made it stand out in a crowded car park, so I had no difficulty finding where I'd left it. More importantly, the car was in excellent condition and also a reasonable price. At last I had my independence in every sense of the word – what more could I want?

17

The Bump and Italians in White Coats

After living on our own for three months, the inevitable happened. I suddenly started feeling nauseous and lost my appetite, which was bad news – I never missed a meal. It could mean only one thing – I was pregnant. Although we wanted to start a family we hadn't expected it to happen so soon. The intense heat during July and August did nothing to alleviate my condition. My pregnancy also coincided with my mum and aunt's first visit to Piussogno. We didn't say anything straightaway just in case it was a false alarm but two weeks later, on their last day, we were more than certain and so gave them the news. They were delighted and couldn't wait to tell everyone back home. If our calculations were correct, the baby was due at the end of February. We decided to tell Michele's family the following Saturday evening before the disco opened.

August seemed to go on forever and the nausea, too. I actually had to stay in bed for a couple of days because my lack of appetite made me feel incredibly weak but a constant string of visitors kept me occupied. Aunts and older cousins would sit on the bed and offer me advice as to which remedy I should take to get my appetite back and younger friends would ask if I preferred a boy or a girl.

"What are your favourite names? Have you chosen any in particular?"

If I feigned surprise at not having thought about it, they were quick to give me suggestions. Some names I could hardly pronounce myself, and with others I wasn't sure which gender they represented, still it helped to pass the time.

Michele proved to be a very caring father-to-be. He banned me from doing any hard or strenuous work. Not that I had done anything remotely vigorous before. I mean, I wouldn't count washing the floors or polishing the furniture as being particularly taxing. He watched over me like a hawk and wouldn't let me carry anything he considered heavy. I enjoyed the attention and four months later, I found a new lease of life. I felt much better and looked forward to mealtimes once again. He insisted on giving me rump steak as soon as I could face food again.

"Red meat is exceptionally good for someone in your condition," ... and so it went on.

As I entered the fifth month, my stomach suddenly expanded overnight and a definite bulge appeared. Within a couple of days the entire village knew that the *inglesina* was expecting. I still walked to the shop each morning. I think it would have been too much of a disappointment for the villagers if I had done otherwise.

They would look me up and down and comment on how well pregnancy suited me.

"Yes, you've definitely got more colour in your cheeks and the extra weight you've put on is just what you needed. You were far too thin before," they nodded to me and muttered to each other in dialect.

I bit my lip and tried hard not to laugh but at the same time I was touched – they were already treating me as one of them.

*

"Where's the maternity clinic?" I asked Michele after Mum had reminded me in her letter that it was time I went for a check-up.

"There isn't one," Michele told me. "I'll take you to the local doctor at Traona."

Not knowing where it was, Michele had to accompany me and for some unknown reason I suddenly felt very vulnerable and very foreign. The surgery was a small room next to the post office. Chairs lined the walls and a pile of magazines sat on a low table in the centre. We took our seats next to a middle-aged couple and it wasn't long before the place was packed.

"Where's the receptionist?" I whispered to Michele.

"There isn't one," he replied.

With no one to call the patients one at a time, it was a free-for-all when someone came out of the doctor's surgery; I couldn't believe how agile most of the elderly people were when it came to jumping the queue. After an hour and a half, we decided that it must be our turn now and Michele stationed himself at the door. This tactic did not deter one old lady who said she had to speak to the doctor as quickly as possible and wrestled past us as soon as the door opened.

When we finally walked inside the surgery, we found the doctor wrapped in a cloud of smoke. He cheerfully puffed on his cigarette before offering us a seat. Now, I've grown up with the knowledge that *Smoking Damages Your Health!* Yet, here was the local GP practically glorifying the vice. I glanced at Michele but he was already trying to make himself comfy on one of the hard metal chairs, obviously a deterrent against lonely people who just wanted an excuse to chat to someone.

The physician continued smoking regardless of the fact that a pregnant woman was sitting opposite him. What kind of doctor was he? Did he not share the ethics of those in the medical profession who scorned expectant mothers who smoked? Didn't he realise that passive smoking is just as harmful to the foetus? What about his patients in general, not everyone is partial to the smell of tobacco? Maybe it was his way of staving off germs, who knows?

I couldn't help staring at him. He was a big man in his fifties with a thick head of black wavy hair and a pair of horn-rimmed glasses perched on his nose. But, despite his grim face, he appeared to have a kindly disposition. He took one look at my *bump* and asked me how many weeks pregnant I was.

"*Hai fatto le analisi?*" He asked in terse Italian. Without waiting for a reply, he picked up a pen between two nicotine-stained fingers and started writing a number of tests for me to do at Morbegno Hospital. Trying hard not to breathe in the smoke, I answered as best I could with Michele translating for me when I got stuck.

"*Torni quando avrà l'esito.*" He spoke slowly enabling me to understand everything he said. Then he turned to Michele and gave him directions to the midwife's home.

Funnily enough, I came out of the surgery coughing. It was a mystery that none of the other patients before me had been affected. They were obviously used to the smoke-filled room and being an avid smoker, Michele suffered no discomfort whatsoever apart from a great longing to light up himself.

We decided to go to the midwife *who lived three villages down the road from us* – excellent directions. We found Pina in her garden, on her knees, pulling up weeds. As she straightened up, I saw a tall, robust woman in her sixties. She had a mane of unruly grey hair and an endearing smile that made me feel relaxed in her company. Fortunately, she showed no signs of cravings for tobacco.

As she bustled us into her house, she asked Michele where we lived and who his parents were. I interpreted this as just a formality but to the inhabitants of these small villages, it was of the utmost importance. She nodded happily when she recognised their names and realised we lived locally. She settled us in the lounge, before excusing herself and disappearing into the bathroom to freshen up, all the while asking questions about my pregnancy that Michele had to answer as she tended to lapse into dialect quite frequently.

Checking her hands to make sure she'd scrubbed them sufficiently, she showed us into a small room that she used to examine her patients and I gingerly lay down on the couch. From her collection of medical instruments, she extracted a wooden object resembling an egg holder. I looked at Michele for reassurance but he was too absorbed watching Pina. She put the *tool* to her ear and then bent over and put the other end on my stomach, moving it slowly over my bump. She then gently felt my stomach. With a smile, she assured me that the baby was growing well and was probably a boy.

"*Sì, sì, è sicuramente un bell' Alpino*", referring to the mountain soldiers who had to do their military service at the age of nineteen. This was considered *un onore*. Whether this was standard talk for the benefit of the father-to-be or it really was *an honour,* I shall never know. What I shall always remember is Michele's face as we walked to the car. He had the biggest smile I'd ever seen. My face was less radiant – what if we had a daughter, would this be considered less *honourable*? So long as the baby was healthy, to me the gender was irrelevant. The *Valtellinesi* wanted male heirs to carry on the family name. I had never heard such chauvinism before in my life and secretly hoped that our firstborn would be a girl. Village life didn't always agree with me.

*

Michele took me to my hospital appointments and the months passed without any complications except for a dull ache in one of my molars. Although I pretended it was all in the mind and eventually it would go away – it didn't. I had to admit that I needed a dentist. For once, I longed for my English dentist, Mr Nicholls, who knew about my foibles when it came to sitting on the couch and opening my mouth. He knew exactly how to stop the trembling before he could make an inspection.

Michele's sister, Anna suggested I made an appointment with her dentist in a nearby town. When I hesitated, she said she would do it for me. The following week, Pietro took me to the dental surgery because Michele had to meet a rep and it was too far for me to walk. As I climbed out of the car, he said he'd pick me up in a couple of hours. I laughed, thinking he was joking.

My appointment was for 2.30 pm but when I walked into the waiting room, I was surprised to see half a dozen people there. After a few minutes, a woman asked me what time I was supposed to see the dentist. When I told her, she said her appointment was also for that time and another two patients said theirs were, too. Either this dentist was the first to perform miracles or we were in for a long wait. Half an hour later, the door opened and a teenage girl walked out wearing a brace.

A very young, glamorous dental assistant came out to call in the next patient. I saw that here there was a different regime and I wouldn't have a ten minute wait at the most as was the case at my dental surgery in Poole. So, I picked up a magazine from the pile on the table and settled down to read it. Nearly two hours later, I had finished it and had just chosen a second one when my name was called. At least, I presumed it was me.

"*Backer Valeria*?" As is the custom in Italy, my maiden name was called, but why was it so difficult to pronounce the word Baker?

"*Sì*," I answered, wishing I were anywhere but there.

The model-like assistant showed me into the surgery and invited me to take my place on the couch. Her make-up was perfect, her hair styled in a way that I was sure only a professional could master, and her white overall only barely covered an enviable cleavage. She glided along on long, slender tanned legs, neatly encased in a pair of elegant high-heeled shoes. A waft of Chanel invaded my nostrils as she tied a plastic bib around my neck. Before I had time to conjure up an image of the dentist, a strong smell of expensive aftershave announced the entrance from a secondary door of a tall, middle-aged man who reminded me of Dr Kildare. He was good-looking and he knew it. Maybe I jumped to an unfair conclusion but I got the feeling that had the assistant been short and frumpy, she'd be working elsewhere.

After a few basic questions, the dentist asked me to open my mouth and he quickly found the offending molar. I had expected him to give me a filling there and then as my faithful English dentist would have done. But no, instead he gave me a long-winded version of the treatment I needed, half of which was far too technical for me to understand, and told me to go back the following week. He advised me to take an aspirin if the pain became unbearable. I couldn't believe it. I'd waited two hours only to be told which one was the bad tooth (as if I didn't know!) and to go back again in a few days to have it treated. I came out holding an appointment card and when Pietro saw my expression, he couldn't help laughing. I had arrived at the dental surgery with toothache and I was going home not just with toothache but with a headache as well.

My next visit wasn't that different. This time I took a book to read as I knew I'd have another long wait – and I did. When the same attractive young woman called me, I braced myself for the ordeal ahead. I fought back the shaking and tried to focus on something positive. The designer-type bib positioned theatrically round my neck and the ornamental mouthwash at my elbow did little to alleviate my state of mind. As the drill found its target, I attempted to find solace in the fact that my tooth would soon be as good as new. Unfortunately, I still had a lot to learn.

The drilling stopped as quickly as it had started and the dentist told me to rinse my mouth. He then inserted a round wad of something resembling cotton wool in the brand new cavity and told me to make another appointment for the following week, advising me to take painkillers if necessary. This dentist obviously had shares in the pharmaceutical field, as well. I came out clutching yet another card. If my English dentist had behaved in a similar fashion, I was sure he'd be out of business by now.

That evening, when I complained to Michele that at this rate the baby would be here before my tooth had been fixed, he laughed and explained that everything takes time and I needed to be patient. However, when I mentioned that he probably wouldn't be laughing when we were given the bill, he realised that we had forgotten to ask for an estimate. He decided to accompany me on my next visit.

As I lay comfortably stretched out on the couch and the cotton wool ball had been removed, the dentist decided he had to take a few x-rays because the tooth had to be *devitalised* or as we would normally say, it had to have the root taken out. I asked him in halting Italian, if it was really necessary to go to such lengths – wouldn't a filling suffice?

"*No, affatto* ," he assured me. I gathered it wouldn't.

At this point, I asked if Michele could join us. If I surprised the dentist by this request, he didn't show it. Michele quizzed him on what treatment I needed and more importantly, what the final cost would be. The dentist did a few sums on his calculator and gave a total to Michele, adding that I might need treatment on other teeth as well. Michele shrugged in a way that only true Italians know how, and took out his chequebook. In turn, the dentist dramatically waved his arms around saying that payment was expected at the end of treatment and not before.

Miss Hollywood, as I'd nicknamed the assistant, ushered Michele back into the waiting room and I had an x-ray taken. As I'd feared, it was deemed more than necessary to have the roots taken out. *Dr Charming* gave me a temporary filling and – you've guessed – another appointment.

"Can't it be done now?" I almost wailed.

The dentist explained that no way could he do it there and then because it was too long a process and I needed a longer appointment. The dental surgery closed for three weeks during August, so I had to go back at the beginning of September. I was more than glad to have a break, though.

I resumed my dental trips the following month and tried very hard to be brave but nothing could quell my fears. I hated the surgery and everything it represented. I continued to shake and subconsciously shut my mouth each time I had to keep it wide open. At one point, the dentist decided to resort to more drastic measures in order to finish his job in hand, and with a flourish and a flowery explanation of what he intended doing, he produced a metal contraption to keep my mouth open. I thought the age of such torture was long gone.

The extraction of the roots proved more complicated than anticipated. Not even the music in the background could distract me. My gut feeling that the dentist tolerated me was enhanced by the fact that he usually managed to time a break for a cigarette during my sitting. Not that I complained because it meant that I could close my mouth and dream that I was somewhere far away with perfect teeth and in no need of a dentist.

*

"Ow! What was that?" I felt the baby move and regardless of whether it was a boy or a girl – this baby

201

had an exceptionally strong kick. When I told Michele, it heightened speculation that it had to be a boy and now, not only Michele went around grinning but Alberto did, too.

My mother-in-law suggested that I should start knitting some clothes for the baby. Being allergic to knitting needles, I hadn't even considered actually making anything. I assumed we'd buy the clothes. Still, I dutifully bought two pairs of knitting needles and balls of baby wool from the village shop. I also chose the easiest knitting pattern available. I couldn't wait to get home in order to begin but my enthusiasm evaporated when I had difficulty keeping the stitches on the needles. After a week of trial and error, I decided to go downstairs and ask Nanda for help. She was only too willing to give me a hand. The only problem was how she held her knitting needles. She literally tucked them under her armpits. I'd already seen my mother-in-law and her sister at work and they too used the same style but I found it impossible to knit this way. Apart from feeling very uncomfortable I didn't seem to make any progress. When Nanda offered to make us a cup of tea, I jumped at the idea and put my knitting away before she'd even got out of her chair, I told her I'd wait for my mum to finish the little vest. I much preferred to have a chat over a cuppa than get stressed over tangled pieces of wool.

While sipping our tea, Baby-B (short for Baby-Barona) kicked and Nanda couldn't help remarking on the strength of it. I told her that the villagers took delight in predicting the baby's sex.

"Sì, sì. E' come una palla. Sicuramente, avrai un maschietto."

They all decided unanimously that my bump was definitely a ball shape and therefore a boy. Had it been pointed, it would be a girl. To my surprise, Nanda suggested that they could be right.

The villagers regularly quizzed me on the names we'd chosen but I decided to keep them guessing. They also checked the calendar to see when the moon changed. Apparently it would indicate the imminent birth. I put it down to *old wives' tales* but, nevertheless, I made a mental note of the date.

A month before my due date, Michele and I went to buy a pram, a pushchair and a cot. Without meaning to, I chose the best and most expensive make. Well, I didn't intend having only one child anyway. I never stopped marvelling at how Italian shops presented their products; window displays beckoned you to go in and buy and everything spelt *design*. Cheap shops just didn't exist here.

The last weeks of my pregnancy proved to be the longest and it didn't help when one of the villagers greeted me every day with the mantra: *"Non è ancora ora?"* I usually answered with a smile that, *no, it wasn't time yet*, but I'm afraid I forgot myself on one occasion, and with tongue in cheek, I told her that the English usually had pregnancies lasting eleven months. She grinned, acknowledging the joke – or so I thought. The next day the entire village had heard that English mothers had to carry their babies for an extra two months compared to the rest of the world. Michele didn't see the funny side of it and I vowed never again to make such a facetious remark. Mind you, I never for one moment expected the woman to take me seriously.

18

It's a Boy!

My mum arrived a week before the baby was due to give me moral support. My due date came and went. My birthday passed insignificantly and the following week we celebrated Sofia's ninth birthday downstairs. I was already ten days late.

The day after Sofia's party, I found a new reserve of energy and cleaned the flat from top to bottom. I caught Mum eyeing me with a knowing look.

"Have you prepared your bag for the hospital?"

Naturally, the bag had been sitting in a corner of the bedroom for ages.

That evening, I was very restless and didn't feel like going to bed, preferring to play cards even if Michele won each game – and then it happened – my waters broke and Mum suggested I went to hospital.

In the maternity ward, a gynaecologist examined me and said that the birth was imminent but after a few hours she sent Michele home. He didn't want to leave me because there was no means of contacting him. We didn't have a telephone in the flat. She assured him that the baby wouldn't be delivered before the morning and settled me in a room with three beds with a 21 year old who had had a baby girl that day. Seeing that I was in no immediate pain and could make myself reasonably understood with the hospital staff, Michele went home.

In the early hours of the morning, a young girl arrived and, as she lay in the middle bed, I soon forgot my own discomfort, hearing her shouting:

"*Madonna, Madonna! O Madonna, aiutami!*" Her pleading was so sincere that I really hoped Mary was listening to her and would help her. At one point, she turned to me and uttered something unintelligible.

"I'm sorry, but I can't understand what you're saying. I'm English," I told her in my best Italian. This was greeted with what I can only suppose was a torrent of abuse. I did the sensible thing for once and pressed the button for a nurse. Good job, too. After taking one look at her, the nurse called for her colleagues and wheeled her into the delivery room. Heart-wrenching screams filled the corridors followed by a baby's defiant cry, then an emphatic silence. Half an hour later, she was back in bed next to me, sleeping peacefully, her daughter safely in her cot in the hospital's crèche or *nido* as it was called here.

Michele came to see me later that morning and we chatted until a nun, who was also a nurse, sent him home for lunch.

"You're far too thin. Go home and eat something," she told him and not wanting to argue with her, he left.

After yet another examination, the doctor decided to

take me through to the delivery room as it seemed that things *might* be moving. The best thing about your first child is that you are blissfully ignorant as to what's going to happen – or so it was in my case. I had been given numerous books on preparing for birth and made a conscientious effort to read at least one but I just couldn't get further than page 23 on the chapter referring to contractions and breathing. My motto being I'd cross that bridge when I came to it.

The hospital staff couldn't have been kinder and the consultant made a special concession for me, allowing Michele to come any time in case I had problems regarding the language barrier. He apologized for the fact that babies were kept in the *nido* and not in a cot by the mother's side as was the case in England. A young student doctor stayed by my side to monitor the baby's progress. He appeared more anxious than me and to lighten the atmosphere I said I'd like to talk.

"Sei mai stata a un concerto Pop a Londra?" he asked.

I told him I'd gone to the all-day pop concert at Wembley in 1975. He knew all about it and asked what I'd thought of the various singers. The contractions came and went amid memories of that unforgettable day. Now and again he'd interrupt me to check on the baby then he'd make himself comfy and say: *"Continua..."* and so I'd continue, occasionally gripping the bed rail when yet another labour pain wracked my body. When the gynaecologist popped in to see us and asked at what point we were, I was afraid the doctor was going to say: "Elton John has just finished his medley."

Instead, he said very professionally, that there was no change.

Both Mum and Michele came to see me in the afternoon and stayed until the nun shooed them out again.

"We'll be back later," Michele promised but I was past caring, I just wanted to get on with the birth. The young doctor shifted uneasily on his chair as another spasm tore through me. During the afternoon and early evening, three other women had come in and given birth to daughters. At one point, the nun had told Michele he was the father of a baby girl then she realised a few minutes later that it wasn't his. I could just imagine the nun rushing out in a flurry of white skirts saying:

"You've got a beautiful baby girl!" Then two minutes later:

"No, you haven't. It's not yours." Poor Michele. He'd suffered as well.

Finally, my baby decided to make his way into the world.

"*E'un maschietto!*" The doctor told me, as he washed and examined my baby before whisking him away to the *nido*. The young doctor went out to tell Michele that he was at last the father of a baby boy. Mum, too could relax now. Back in the room, they allowed me to see them for a few minutes. Then Michele took Mum home before going to the disco with the news. Everyone had free drinks that Friday evening because I'd given birth to a baby boy at 7.15pm, weighing 9lbs 4ozs, and 52 centimetres long. Not bad. I fell asleep feeling ecstatically happy in my new role of mother.

The following morning I introduced myself to the two other occupants in the room. The girl who had apparently sworn at me was very contrite but the nurses assured us it's quite common at such a delicate time.

It had been suggested that I spoke Italian to my baby to avoid confusing him. My Italian vocabulary wasn't rich enough to explain that a child from the age of 0 to 7 is like a sponge, soaking up information and has no trouble whatsoever in learning languages. Michele and I had already discussed the subject of languages and we decided that from day one I would speak English and he would speak Italian. That way my family would have no problem communicating and our child would be bi-lingual. When I first set eyes on Alex, it was absolutely impossible for me to speak to him in a foreign language. How on earth was I supposed to say: *"Ciao, amore. Come sei bello!"* (Hello, my love. You're beautiful!) It was unnatural.

When the nurses brought our babies to feed, Alex seemed huge compared to the others. He sucked contentedly and then fell asleep. Medical staff and neo-mothers listened fascinated as I chatted away in English to my baby. Thirty years ago, French was still the second language; English fever had yet to come.

"Che cosa stai dicendo?" They asked, and I'd have to translate.

"Dai, dillo ancora!" and I'd have to repeat what I'd just said.

"Ah, che bello!" and they'd sigh in awe to think that a new-born baby was already learning two languages.

Surprisingly enough, I didn't have that much trouble making myself understood. Occasionally, medical terms would throw me, but by gesticulating all was revealed. The first morning, however, when the nurse came round with a thermometer I automatically started to put it under my tongue.

"*No, no, no! Mettilo qui!*" she said, pretending to put one under her left armpit. I had no idea that Italians took their temperature that way. I obediently did as I was told but it slipped down when I nodded off and I had to have a quick search for it under the bedclothes when she came to collect it. Breakfast was served at an unearthly hour, so it came as no surprise to me when two more nurses appeared a few hours later each holding a kettle. Unfortunately, it wasn't to give us a cup of tea as I had thought but to disinfect our stitches. I remember thinking that they could have used a different container. One of the nurses wanted to know why I had stopped smiling. She couldn't help laughing when I explained and immediately told her colleague in dialect, who then remembered the incident with the thermometer.

"*Che carina!*" said the nurse who was called Clara. I'd heard the phrase often but hadn't a clue what it meant. I had to wait for Michele to enlighten me.

"It means: 'ow sweet!" said my husband later. I should have known it was something like that.

I had no end of visitors who naturally wanted to see the latest member of the Barona clan. Together we walked down the corridor to the *nido* and peered through the glass at the babies in their cots side by side.

One man whose wife still had to give birth, told her to give him a son like *number 7*. Michele couldn't have felt prouder when he realised that the man was referring to Alex.

I had to stay in hospital for over a week because the birth was considered a difficult one and although I'd rather have gone home as soon as possible, the rest did me good. All the nurses and doctors spoke slowly making sure that I understood what they had said. The nun, however, made no concessions for me and one morning gave me a right telling off along with the others because our bedside cabinets were too untidy. I obediently put everything inside the locker out of sight and was rewarded with one of her rare smiles.

On the day I took Alex home, I realised that I hadn't changed him, bathed him or even dressed him once. In fact, he was the first baby I had really held for any length of time. I had no recollections of my younger brother or sister as babies, apart from my grandmother giving me a Bourbon biscuit – my favourite – when they were born at home. My four cousins had grown up in London and Cornwall and during their early years, we met up only on festive occasions. The doctors and nurses took it for granted that my maternal instincts would come to the fore and waved us goodbye without giving me any helpful hints on how to look after a newborn baby.

I needn't have worried. Together with Michele and my mum, I coped. Anyway, being a naturally contented baby, Alex only cried when he was hungry or needed changing.

We were a bit anxious about our landlord Luigi being woken up in the night when Alex cried for his last feed because as a long distance lorry driver, he had to invariably get up in the early hours of the morning. He soon put our minds at rest, though by saying that he only heard a very faint cry and it made him feel young again.

We were inundated with people coming to see the new baby and I couldn't help feeling slightly peeved when relatives came and automatically lifted Alex out of the pram regardless of whether he was sleeping at the time. My protectiveness towards my son verged on obsessiveness; it suddenly became all-important to me to give him an English upbringing, which is fine if you're living in Poole but presents difficulties if you're living in Piussogno.

Two days after we brought Alex home, at the tender age of ten days, Mum and I found him sitting on Michele's lap watching a sports programme. As Michele explained the highlights of the Fiorentina match to him, I knew my son was destined to support a team that would make him suffer like his father before him.

On Alex's first outing in his pram, it seemed that the entire village just happened to be out, too. Sleeping peacefully, he was thankfully oblivious to the endless stream of faces stuck in front of him.

"Che bel bambino! Cresce bene?"

"Assomiglia a suo papà, vero?"

"E' bravo, mangia, dorme?"

They ricocheted questions at me which I answered as best I could, telling them that yes, he'd put on weight;

212

yes, he looked just like his father; yes, he was very good, he ate well and slept through the night. Ignoring the fact that no one had said he looked like me.

*

The next important event was the christening. We wanted to baptise Alex before Mum went back to Poole, so Don Giulio suggested a date six weeks after Alex's birth. The only minor discrepancy being that we had to christen him *Alessandro* because the Church wouldn't accept the name Alex. To all other intents and purposes, though, he was Alex and we registered him in that name. We bought light blue coloured sugar almonds for the occasion and Michele's aunt crocheted some beautiful blue swans in which to put the *confetti*, as the sweets are called. We gave Mum a batch to take home for the English relatives.

Choosing godparents proved a problem. Michele's family was Catholic and mine was Protestant. Godparents, thirty years ago, had to be Catholic. We didn't think it would be fair to ask Michele's brother and sisters and not mine. So we compromised and asked Michele's cousin and her husband to be godmother and godfather. With that sorted, we could sit back and enjoy the preparations for the Christening. Michele's sister and her boyfriend gave us a beautiful christening gown for Alex with a matching cushion to lay him on. I had to buy a new outfit for the occasion and Mum happily agreed to accompany me, an afternoon in Morbegno proving a welcome diversion from the solitary walks with a pram around Piussogno where pavements still had to make their debut. With Alex sleeping peacefully, and two and a half hours before his next feed, we went to a boutique where I'd already bought several items of clothing. In my best Italian I explained what I needed to the assistant, and then, having assessed my size, she flapped around the shop, selecting possible outfits. One by one, I tried them on. Being Pisces made the choice more difficult, I just couldn't make up my mind between a blue dress and a cream suit. In the end I decided on the dress and as we walked out of the shop, Mum breathed a sigh of relief. She was in dire need of a strong cup of tea.

A few days before the Christening, we ordered a special cake that would be eaten in the afternoon after the service. The day before the Baptism, we went to a florist to buy some flowers to decorate the church. The floral arrangements were exquisite, and naturally, expensive. I had to pretend that I could only remember the names of flowers in English, such was my ignorance regarding flora. I still had to develop green fingers.

As our car had to have its MOT that day, we borrowed Pietro's car to go and fetch the cake in the afternoon, and coming home we decided to stop at a bar for a quick *cappuccino*. Michele opened the car door and as I climbed in I realised the cake was missing.

"Where's the cake?"

"Where's my jacket?" cried Mum.

"Oh, no!" said Michele. "It's the wrong car!"

A red, Alfa Romeo car, exactly the same as Pietro's, had parked next to us and we had opened the wrong car door. Michele locked the door again as quickly as possible and then nonchalantly moved round to the *right* car, where the cake was sitting in its designer box on the back seat. We climbed in and sped off still giggling and hoping no one had seen us.

The following day proved a memorable one to say the least. The immediate family and godparents came for lunch – which did not consist of meat and two veg – but a three-course meal, not forgetting cheese and fruit to finish. Naturally, my mother-in-law took charge of the proceedings and on this occasion I quite happily let her choose the menu and help me prepare it.

After clearing up, we changed into our finery and at quarter past two, we walked solemnly down the road to the church where several older members of the community were already sitting in the pews. They never missed a religious event, be it a wedding, baptism or funeral. The two flower arrangements by the altar looked just right and I had to admit that the florist knew what she was talking about when she advised us on which floral decorations to choose.

The priest came to greet us and he said a few words to Alex which I thought was a very sweet gesture. The service was short but meaningful and Don Giulio made sure he didn't frighten Alex when he gently poured holy water over his forehead. In some cases, priests were prone to showering the baby which invariably culminated in the baby screaming hysterically until the service ended. Don

Giulio gave Alex a candle and a little white robe neatly folded in a box as a keepsake.

We gave the traditional sugar almonds to the children who had turned up in the hope of getting a few sweets before Don Giulio joined our procession back to the house for a slice of cake and a glass of red wine.

The party was still in full swing at seven that evening when Michele's mum discreetly asked him what we were going to offer our guests. Now feeling quite tired, I had no wish to start cooking over a hot stove.

"I'll go down to Giovanna's shop and ask 'er if she could give us some rolls, cold meats and cheeses," Michele whispered to me.

"But it's Sunday. She'll be closed," I reminded him.

"She doesn't go far on 'er day off, so 'opefully I'll find 'er."

And with that, he disappeared. Thirty minutes later, he came back with a carrier bag full of food. I laid up the table once again, the wine flowed and the impromptu buffet was naturally a success.

19

England v Italy

The time came for Mum to go back to Poole and I knew I was going to miss her. We planned to take Alex over in the summer to meet my family; so, at least I had something to look forward to. As soon as Mum left, my in-laws started coming round in the evening just as I'd put Alex to bed. Now it's a well-known fact that the English like to have a routine and I am no exception. One of the first things I noticed when I arrived in Italy was the fact that parents let their babies and children stay up late in the evening. There was no such thing as putting them to bed at seven-thirty regardless of whether they wanted to go or not. It was also unthinkable to put a child in his cot and leave him to cry. No, you had to cradle him until he fell asleep.

I had no intention of allowing my newly born son to stay awake all evening. We put him in his pram in our bedroom and left him to rest. They continued to visit and despite their raised voices in a vain attempt to wake the baby, invariably they were only able to have a quick peep at him fast asleep. I knew I should have been more lenient but I wanted everyone to know that my son was Anglo-Italian.

I didn't suffer from 'baby blues' which was just as well, but I did feel terribly homesick at times. I missed my family and the companionship of a friend to discuss babies or just chat about nothing in particular. At least I had the car – we nicknamed it *Carolina* – and could take Alex for his monthly check-ups myself without having to rely on anybody. Healthcare visitors didn't exist in Italy and it was up to the parents to take their baby to a paediatrician at the nearest hospital. I made our appointments at the one in Morbegno and this time, I didn't stare open mouthed when white-coated doctors walked up and down the corridors drawing deeply on their cigarettes, leaving a puffy haze behind them. I came to the conclusion they must have shares in tobacco companies.

Alex was four months old when he had his first official photograph taken for his identity card and then a few weeks later, he flew to England for the first time. Of course, a lot of people considered us mad, cruel even, to contemplate taking a baby on a plane but we had preferential treatment on the flight with a carrycot for Alex to sleep in. He seemed to take everything in his stride and never cried.

He was an obvious hit with his English relations and his great-grandparents were delighted with the latest member of the family. He had his first rusk and baby food in Poole. Despite the cooler weather, we still took Alex to the beach and let him paddle in the English

Channel. He loved it. The sea air did him the world of good but of course, nothing could beat Sandbanks, the Chines and Canford Cliffs, anyway.

Back in Piussogno, our lives followed a familiar pattern and I only really longed for my *old* life when the bottled gas ran out on a Saturday night in the middle of cooking our meal or when the big one we shared with the Gusmeroli family finished while I was washing my hair. Apart from that, you could say I was reasonably contented. One drawback was that I still had molar problems. Alex was born just after the first tooth had been restored to its former self but instead of saying goodbye to the dentist, I suddenly found I had a lack of calcium and more teeth were giving me problems. I resigned myself to the fact that I was going to be a regular patient at the dental surgery whether I liked it or not. For my own peace of mind, I decided to ignore the fact that it had taken nearly five months to fix one tooth. All of a sudden, the dentist was inundated with emergencies and my appointments were left longer. Instead of weekly visits, I now made monthly ones but as I wasn't suffering from excruciating toothache, it didn't matter.

Unfortunately, I wasn't the only one having dental problems; Alex developed a high temperature and bronchitis with every tooth he cut. The first time it happened, Carla arrived as I rocked my fractious, seven month old baby in my arms trying to soothe him. Touching his forehead, she told me to fetch the thermometer and nearly had an apoplectic fit when I explained that we didn't have one. Well aware that he felt hotter than usual, I hadn't considered it to be life-threatening but Carla's quick fire barrage of questions as to what I'd done or more to the point, hadn't done, managed to reduce me to an agitated state of total incoherence. Five minutes later, I found myself standing inside the chemist's at Traona buying a thermometer and making enquiries as to what I could give Alex to alleviate his pain. The pharmacist assured me that his condition was a common one when teething and not to worry. I came home feeling calmer. At such times, I missed not having my mum or sister around terribly.

*

Alex was our pride and joy. He grew from a happy, gurgling baby into an inquisitive toddler. He took his first steps at Cercino, on one of our visits to see Emily and Nino, when he was one. Just as if I'd wound him up like a clockwork toy, he suddenly stood up and staggered from one room to the next, grinning as he discovered he could move by himself. Six months later he started talking. He was used to hearing Mummy speak English and *Papà parlare in Italiano*. Consequently, he chose the easiest words from both languages.

"Mummy, I want *la pappa*," he'd say when he wanted his food. As he grew older, he learnt to switch languages depending on whom he was talking to. Not everyone liked me speaking to Alex in English, but the comments fell on deaf ears.

"*Che cosa gli stai dicendo?*" they quizzed me.

"I just asked him if he wanted to go for a walk."

His English roots would never be forgotten – especially when it came to bringing him up. I had no intention of raising a spoilt child who thought the world revolved around him, so I preferred to ignore the raised eyebrows and muttering. Rules were rules and he had to learn them: books were for reading, not scribbling on; toys had to be put away when he'd finished playing with them; he couldn't have everything he wanted; he had to say 'please' and 'thank you'. This seemed to be too much for the Italians – I shouldn't be so strict with such a young child, being a mother meant letting him learn for himself and enjoy life. He would be traumatised by such a regime. Not to be deterred, I smiled sweetly at my son when he'd done something wrong and, speaking quietly in English, told him to rectify it immediately if he didn't want a smacked bottom. It worked every time – and no one was any the wiser.

I dressed him alternatively in clothes from Mothercare in Poole, which brought showers of compliments, and outfits from a revered Baby shop in Morbegno. He became a familiar sight pulling his treasured toy, a Fisher Price Spotty Dog behind him when we went out walking. He loved going to the disco and playing on the dance floor. As soon as Michele put a record on and switched on the lights above it, he would run in circles trying to catch the fragments of flashing colours reflected on the floor. When he was tired, he'd sit down and watch the central light turn round and round. Then after a few minutes he'd stand up again and start dancing. He had music in his blood, no doubt about that.

About this time, I became friendly with an English girl who lived with her Italian boyfriend in Morbegno and worked in a travel agency. Alex began calling her Auntie Kathy and we'd meet up on her day off and sometimes on a Sunday afternoon when Michele was busy at the disco. She had carpet throughout the house and had actually managed to grow gooseberries in her garden which reminded me of home. We'd reminisce over a cup of English tea, while Alex kicked a ball around the garden and played with Prince, her adorable collie. Like me, she missed a lot of English products and each time she went back home to England, she'd take an empty case so that she could bring back a supply of baked beans, custard, tea bags etc. I followed her example on future trips. Occasionally, we'd drive down to the lake and enjoy the sunshine; other times we'd walk along the river Adda with Prince tugging on his lead and Alex in his pushchair. Together we moaned about shop opening hours, hoping that one day they would adapt to the British way and at times, we complained about the mentality of the *Valtellinesi*. They could be incredibly narrow-minded. Men still expected their wives to stay home and look after them and their offspring, whereas they thought nothing of spending all their free time at the bar, chatting with their cronies over a card game of *briscola* or *scala quaranta*. Fortunately, Michele didn't come under that category – even so, he still went to the bar on a Tuesday night to meet his friends and play cards. Men were, and in my opinion will always be, very attached to their mothers. *La mamma* is very much the central figure. I made a resolution that Alex would definitely *not* be a Mummy's Boy.

Tina, one of Michele's twin cousins, took to coming regularly in the afternoon to see us. Alex idolised her and it was reciprocal.

"*Devo stirare per te?*" she'd ask, if she saw a pile of clothes ready and waiting to be ironed.

"*No, no, è…*" before I had time to finish she had filled the iron and plugged it in to *de-crease* the clothes. She also had a knack of calming Alex when he was teething and so to show my appreciation for her help, we invited her to stay for meals. I introduced her to various English dishes and her favourites were shepherd's pie and apple crumble with custard. Whereas Tina always had time to look after Alex in the afternoon when she'd done her homework, my mother-in-law divided her days inside the kitchen cooking and outside digging or pruning. This meant she could only look after her grandson if it rained or the elements forced her to stay indoors. Unfortunately, I nearly always got the timing wrong and needed her help when the sun shone in a cloud-free sky and the serious business of working the land beckoned her.

*

When school reopened in September, I very often passed the primary school in the village during break-time. As soon as Michele's cousins spotted me with the pushchair,

223

they rushed over to the fence to speak to me while their friends watched with big round eyes and mouths agape when I spoke to Alex in English. They all wore the regulation black overalls; the girls had frilly, white collars, over their everyday clothes. I only ever saw one teacher with them, who in fact had taught Michele. Mind you, the numbers weren't exactly high – I counted about eleven children, varying in height. Michele told me that the children were taught altogether in one class, not an easy feat for one teacher. I wondered whether Alex would have to attend a mixed-level primary school class or more to the point, did I want him to?

Having a child of my own, I became acutely aware of how Italian children were treated as mini adults and even included in family discussions, often quite heated ones. I got the impression that they were left very much to their own devices because so many people remarked on the fact that I sat on the rug with Alex and played with him. I couldn't think of anything more natural than amusing my son. Watching him playing with his toys and then smiling up at me, I knew I wanted the very best for him. Again the seeds of doubt started sprouting in my mind – what did Piussogno have to offer? No pavements, no park, no play area. Now Poole…

Epilogue

Another year drew steadily to an end and looking out of the window I could see sprays of colour as fireworks lit up the shadowy mountains. Listening to the presenter on the television shouting the countdown to 1981, I smiled to myself, ruminating over life and the surprises it held for us.

The disco flourished, Michele prospered, Alex thrived and I clung to the vision that maybe I could adapt and be happy in this godforsaken mountain village after all. That is, until something triggered off a hidden memory or a comment relating to the future made me sit up and think. Once again, my head reeled from conflicting notions, and I knew I still had to make up my mind as to where my home really was.

Oh, yes, I loved my husband and my son unconditionally, I relished the breath-taking sight of the Alps from our balcony, I enjoyed the quiet walks in the woods or along the lake which compensated for the frenetic lifestyle of the city I'd left behind and I valued the friends I'd made here – but still something was missing. While wrestling with my conscience, I found I was pregnant with our second child and I knew I had to make a decision; would the baby be born in Italy or England? That's another story...